JENNIFER LOPEZ

Actor and Singer

James Robert Parish

Ferguson Publishing
An imprint of Infobase Publishing

Jennifer Lopez: Actor and Singer

Ferguson
An imprint of Infobase Publishing
132 West 31st Street
New York NY 10001

Library of Congress Cataloging-in-Publication Data
Parish, James Robert.
  Jennifer Lopez : actor and singer / James Robert Parish
    p. cm.
  Includes index.
  ISBN 0-8160-5832-6 (alk. paper)
  1. Lopez, Jennifer, 1970—Juvenile literature. 2. Actors—United States—Biography—Juvenile literature. 3. Singers—United States—Biography—Juvenile literature. I. Title.
  PN2287.L634P37 2005
  791.43'028'092—dc22   2005011187

Ferguson books are available at special discounts when purchased in bulk quantities for businesses, associations, institutions, or sales promotions. Please call our Special Sales Department in New York at (212) 967-8800 or (800) 322-8755.

You can find Ferguson on the World Wide Web at http://www.fergpubco.com

Text design by David Strelecky

Pages 91–127 adapted from Ferguson's *Encyclopedia of Careers and Vocational Guidance, Thirteenth Edition*

Printed in the United States of America

MP JT 10 9 8 7 6 5 4 3 2 1

This book is printed on acid-free paper.

CONTENTS

1

THE REAL JENNIFER LOPEZ

In the late 1990s and the early years of the new millennium, movie star/recording artist Jennifer Lopez was in the media spotlight. Much of the attention was focused on her dramatic private life. During this time Jennifer was twice married and divorced. Then, in June 2004, she wed again.

As Jennifer's shifting relationships played out before the world, it was easy for the public to overlook how much she had accomplished professionally. Jennifer performed as a dancer and an actor on various TV series in the early 1990s, and she enjoyed great critical and popular success in her breakthrough movie role in *Selena* (1997). Jennifer was paid $1 million for her work in that film. That impressive salary made her the highest-paid female Latin performer in the history of Hollywood. Jennifer's fee per picture soon jumped to $2 million for *Out of Sight* (1998), to $4 million for *The Cell* (1999), and to $9 million for *The Wedding Planner* (2001). Later, her acting income would rise further. It escalated to $12 million for 2002's *Maid in Manhattan* and to $15 million for 2005's *Monster-in-Law*.

While Jennifer's movie career was taking off, she decided to return to one of her first creative loves—music. Her debut album, *On the 6* (1999), was filled with a vibrant Latin flavor that came from Jennifer's Puerto Rican–American roots. The well-received album rose to the number eight position on the *Billboard* album chart. Her follow-up release, *J.Lo* (2001), quickly achieved the top spot on the *Billboard* album sales tabulations.

Jennifer's initial music-industry popularity came as part of a so-called "Latin explosion" in the recording business. The late 1990s was a period when Latin performers such as Ricky Martin, Marc Anthony, Christina Aguilera, Enrique Iglesias, Carlos Santana, and Shakira were all capturing the attention of the mainstream public. As Agustin Gurza detailed in the *Los Angeles Times* (August 15, 2004), "Never before had so many Latinos spent so much time at the top of the pop charts in a single year. . . . Suddenly, Latinos were hot and cool at the same time."

While some of the performers involved in this Latin explosion passed in and out of widespread popularity,

Jennifer Lopez retained her appeal as both a recording artist and leading lady in the movies. Meanwhile, like many other superstars, she had branched out in new professional directions. As an energetic, hands-on entrepreneur, her business operations included a clothing line, a fragrance, and a restaurant. Within a few years Jennifer had built her own commercial empire.

With so many facets to Jennifer's success, it was difficult for the media or the public to define her and her career in any one way. Jennifer successfully fought against being stereotyped in her movie roles, so she did not want to be defined by her looks or any single aspect of her career. Always ambitious, Jennifer once said of her many goals in life: "I want everything. I want family. I want to do good work. I want love. I want to be comfortable." She also noted, "I think of people like Cher and Bette Midler and Diana Ross and Barbra Streisand. That's always been the kind of career I'd hoped to have. I want it all."

In rising to and meeting her lofty dreams—especially in the early years—Jennifer had to overcome the career limitations that the American film and TV industries have placed on ethnic minorities. Jennifer had seen how Hollywood had narrowed the professional opportunities for ethnic minorities in the past. As a result, once Jennifer migrated from TV to mainstream Hollywood movies, she

Jennifer Lopez is a successful actor, singer, and entrepreneur.
(Wire Image)

deliberately chose screen assignments that were not ethnic-specific. She did not want to play parts that might be perceived by the public as one-dimensional racial stereotypes.

Through her determination to become part of the mainstream in the American entertainment industry, Jennifer has helped to minimize racial boundaries in show business.

2

MODEST BEGINNINGS

Jennifer Lynn Lopez was born in the Castle Hill section of the Bronx in New York on July 24, 1970 (some sources suggest 1969 as her true birth year). She was the second of three girls (she has an older sister, Leslie, and a younger sister, Lynda) of David and Guadalupe (Lupe) Lopez. Both parents had emigrated from the city of Ponce, Puerto Rico, when they were youngsters and, years later, met in New York City.

The Castle Hill section of the Bronx is a blue-collar residential area of New York. David worked the night shift at the Guardian Insurance Company, later becoming a computer technician at the firm.

When Jennifer was born, the Lopez family was living in a small apartment. A few years later, after much scrimping and saving, Jennifer's parents were able to buy a modest two-story house, also in Castle Hill. The new

Lopez home was across the street from their church, and all three Lopez girls attended the nearby Holy Family School. Jennifer's mother, Lupe, first worked at Holy Family School as a hall monitor. Later, after attending night school, she became a kindergarten teacher at the facility.

The Lopez girls had a well-disciplined life at home and at school. Their parents wanted the children to be well mannered, to faithfully attend church, and to never be late for school. According to Jennifer, "I was a good kid. I was always hugging people. I was very close to my grandparents, and I listened to my mother and didn't do bad things. I didn't curse and I didn't run around. I was never naughty, but I was a tomboy and very athletic."

Looking back on her childhood, Jennifer has strong positive feelings about living in Castle Hill. "It is just like any other inner city. I grew up in what I consider to be a nice neighborhood, and for me it was . . . well, it was normal." Although life in the Bronx could be tough and one always had to be alert when walking through the streets, Jennifer believes that this atmosphere caused her to be more aware, self-protective, and strong in dealing with all aspects of daily life. As she has explained, "Growing up there made Hollywood a piece of cake in a way, because I had the street smarts and sensibility, and I didn't grow up in that [film colony] environment. I also have perspective, because I know what it is to live in the Bronx. . . . " Jennifer realizes that living in such an environment as Castle Hill "doesn't let your head get too in the clouds."

Early Ambitions

As a small child, Jennifer had secret dreams of one day becoming an entertainer. She explains, "I just knew it was something I wanted to do. . . . I always wanted to sing and dance and be in movies, but when you're little, you don't really understand what the 'rich and famous' part is all about—it's just a catchphrase that means 'I wanna be doing what they're doing up there.' And ever since I was three that's how I was—I always felt all this drama inside of me."

Jennifer inherited her love of show business from her mother, who once had ambitions of becoming a professional entertainer herself. A lover of song and dance, Mrs. Lopez was constantly singing and dancing about the house and encouraging her children to put on little performances at home. Jennifer recalls, "We used to do little shows, even if it was just cartwheels. Whatever made them [i.e., the extended family] clap, we did." Sometimes the girls would perform songs from Broadway musicals for an appreciative audience of their relatives.

One of Lupe's favorite films was *West Side Story* (1961), which she made her three daughters watch on TV.

Jennifer, in particular, was immediately drawn to this famous movie musical, which focused on life in New York's Puerto Rican community. As a young girl, she was especially inspired by Rita Moreno, a Puerto Rican–born actress who appears in the film. (Moreno's performance as Anita earned her an Academy Award for Best Actress in a Supporting Role.) Lopez told *People* magazine in March 1997, "There were zero Latinos on TV, so Rita Moreno was

As a young girl, Jennifer was inspired by the musical film West Side Story *and one of its stars, Puerto Rican–born actor Rita Moreno (first woman on the right).* (Photofest)

the only one I identified with." Not seeing any Latino per-formers on television had led Jennifer to conclude, "If you don't see anybody like you there, it's like, 'Well, I guess I don't exist.'"

Over the years, Jennifer would watch *West Side Story* countless times. She always hoped to star one day in a new version of this classic musical. When dreaming of this goal, Jennifer always fantasized about playing Maria, because it was the lead part. Jennifer reasons, "That's the actress in me, wanting to be the center of attention and the star of the show. I just always wanted to achieve and be proud of myself."

Jennifer was also intrigued by other icons of Hollywood's golden age whom she saw on TV. She says, "I grew up watching real movie stars—Ava Gardner, Rita Hayworth, Marilyn Monroe. Glamorous women like those are why I wanted to get into the business." Jennifer adds, "And from the time I first started off as an actress, each day I had an audition, I'd wake up, do my hair and my makeup, look at myself in the mirror and say, 'I have the stardom glow today.'"

One passion in particular that Jennifer shared with her two siblings was their mutual love of the TV series *Charlie's Angels* (1976–81). The program was about a group of three beautiful female detectives whose cases always involved action, mystery, and intrigue. Jennifer and her sisters would often act out the show when they were playing. Sometimes the girls' rambunctious behavior led to outbursts of roughhousing between them, which were often loud enough to be heard from outside the house.

Self-sufficient, ambitious, and full of her own ideas, Jennifer did not always fit in at school. For example, when she was in the fourth grade, Jennifer once became angry when a good friend talked about her behind her back. This led to a schoolyard fight between the girls, with Jennifer emerging as the victor. Having proven that she was not to be taken lightly, the youngster passed through the next years of school without further problems from her classmates. Jennifer was glad that she had stood up for herself, but looking back, she has said she was not proud that it had led to a physical fight: "I've matured since then."

The Budding Dancer

With their mother's encouragement, the three Lopez girls took dancing classes. Jennifer in particular was excited to participate in the lessons, which she took several times weekly after school at the Kips Bay Boys and Girls Club. The club's director, Harold Maldonado Jr., has vivid memories of the future movie star. "There was something about Jennifer and the way she was determined to come here every day, work hard, help out the younger kids. After class, she'd stick around and ask questions. She was so dedicated." The administrator also noted, "Even as a kid, Jennifer always wanted to take on more. She wanted to learn more dance routines, more parts."

The Kips Bay Boys and Girls Club often put on musicals. One of their productions was *My Fair Lady*. Arlene Rodriguez, a classmate and good friend of Jennifer's, remembers, "She played a hobo or a bum, a poor kid, wearing little knickers. She wasn't the star, but she was the one who stood out. She was always good at everything."

Later, Mrs. Lopez enrolled Jennifer at the Ballet Hispanico in Manhattan. Each weekend she drove her daughter to her dance classes.

Looking back at her first taste of show business, Jennifer says, "My mother might have been a little bit of a frustrated actress, but she wasn't a [pushy] stage mom. We went to dance classes every weekend. But it wasn't till I got older that I started to pursue it myself."

In addition to her interest in dance, Jennifer shared her mother's love of music. As a girl her appreciation of songs was wide and varied. According to Jennifer, "I was in third grade when The Sugarhill Gang's 'Rapper's Delight' [one of the first big hits of recorded hip-hop music] changed my life. But then, when I came home, my mother would be listening to Celia Cruz, Tito Puente, or Diana Ross. That's my background. It's what I call Latin soul." Another of the many musical influences in the Lopez household was Barbra Streisand, a favorite of Lupe Lopez. David Lopez particularly liked doo-wop music from the 1950s, but other musical genres, including rock, salsa, and meringue, were also popular listening choices.

Jennifer also put her excess energy to use through athletics. She says, "I'd always be running around and playing sports and stuff. I did gymnastics, [later] competed nationally in track, and was on the school softball team."

For the youngster, the times her mother took her and her sisters into Manhattan to have lunch with their father was a favorite treat. "It was a huge deal. We'd get dressed

Jennifer and her mother, Lupe, in 2004 (Landov)

up, take the train all the way downtown, have lunch, walk around Union Square. We had a whole ritual. It was incredible, seeing things and people and stores we never saw. It was a place where dreams were made, you know? Whereas the Bronx was just where you lived."

Growing Pains

As a mature woman Jennifer Lopez would become a Hollywood sex symbol. But like many adolescents, she went through growing pains and awkward phases. Her parents—especially her mother—were always concerned that their girls might be preyed upon by neighborhood boys. Mrs. Lopez constantly warned her girls to be extra careful, to not draw attention to themselves while out in the neighborhood and, especially, never to be flirtatious with the opposite sex.

The teenage Jennifer had a flair for contemporary fashion and music trends. In the 1980s she was one of the many who became intrigued with the new pop idol, Madonna. According to Jennifer, "I always admired her, liked her music, her sense of style. I like that she changed all the time."

At age 11, Jennifer joined family members on a trip to Puerto Rico, her first visit to her parents' homeland. One incident left a vivid impression on her as a girl. "I went into a store and asked if I could see something. The clerk said, 'Talk to me in Spanish.' I understood Spanish but didn't speak it. She said, 'Aren't you Puerto Rican?' I just ran out of the store. I remember feeling such shame." (Jennifer's parents wanted to assimilate into the American way of life and had stressed the speaking of English at home. It was from her grandparents, who lived nearby, that the Lopez girls learned to understand and speak Spanish.)

When Jennifer was 13 she was involved in a near-fatal traffic accident. She recalls, "A truck carrying compressed gas cylinders hit my mom's car. The only thing that saved my life was the fact that I was bending down tying my shoes in the front seat, because his headlight flew through the windscreen and ended up in the back of the car. It would have smashed my face in. I don't even remember exactly how my nose got fractured, but that's why it looks like it does. People always tell me I look like I was hit with a hammer, but I like my nose. In profile it's good, but if you look straight at me or touch it, you can see the flatness."

It was around that time that Jennifer experienced her first schoolgirl crushes on boys in her class. In the coming years she became more interested in dating (although her future show business career was always her top priority). In the tenth grade she took an interest in David Cruz, a local boy. The couple began dating when Jennifer was 15 and continued doing so for the next nine years.

One of the qualities Jennifer liked best about David was that he appreciated her unique fashion style (for example, she wore sweats and strange-looking hats). He also admired her strong sense of self and that she was not just following the crowd. According to Jennifer, the general attitude of the neighborhood was that anyone who tried anything different, such as exercising, going out for track at school, or experimenting with different fashion styles, was seen as peculiar and viewed with suspicion. Jennifer says, "If people see you striving for things, it threatens them. I was like, 'This two-bit town isn't big enough for me.'" In marked contrast, David was always supportive and understanding of his girlfriend. If people criticized her ambitions of reaching beyond the neighborhood, he would say, "Jennifer has bigger plans."

After graduating from the eighth grade at Holy Family, Jennifer attended Preston High School. Located in the Throgs Neck section of the Bronx and situated on the banks of the East River, Preston was a private college-preparatory Catholic school for young women. To get to school, Jennifer had to take a subway and then transfer to a bus. Attending classes at Preston, which was based in a former mansion that was surrounded by spacious lawns, Jennifer had her first brush with an upscale lifestyle. It sparked her desire to become successful so she could partake in the finer things in life.

At the Preston School, which was run by Catholic nuns, Jennifer and her friends often got into trouble because they did not follow the rigid dress code. Then too, buoyant Jennifer was always singing and dancing in the hallways, which was not considered proper etiquette. Sometimes, such behavior led to after-school detention sessions.

When not participating in extracurricular school activities, especially dancing and choreographing class musical plays such as *Godspell*, Jennifer had a series of part-time jobs after classes. For a while she worked in a clothing store. However, she admits, "I danced too much in the store while I was working" and was fired. In fact, Jennifer acknowledges, "I got fired from so many jobs. I guess I wasn't focused. I had bigger ideas in my mind than working in the local Bronx jeans store." One of her least favorite work experiences was the time she was hired by a "bootleg" perfume store: "People would buy fake Chloe perfume, and they'd spray it all over the store, themselves and me. I was this big, walking stink." Eventually she spent two years at a Bronx law firm where, for $150 a week, she was a file clerk.

The Emerging Young Woman

If Jennifer stood out from her classmates and friends by being ambitious, dedicated to her dance classes in

Manhattan, and eager to sparkle with her own look, she was much like her peers in terms of her crushes on movie stars. As a teenager Jennifer's favorite was Ralph Macchio, the young star of *The Karate Kid* (1984). She saw the movie repeatedly at local theaters and even wrote letters to the actor (although she never mailed them). In a fan's way, Jennifer dreamed that one day she and Macchio would be a real-life couple.

While still at Preston, Jennifer learned about a film that was to be shot in Philadelphia and that required several teenage girls for small parts. She auditioned and was cast in *My Little Girl* (1986). In this dramatic film, Jennifer plays Myra, one of the young women at a center for troubled girls. Although the low-budget film came and went rather quickly in theaters, Jennifer now had a movie performance to her credit.

As Jennifer completed high school, her parents encouraged her to go on to college. They wanted her to become a lawyer. They thought it was time she put aside her passion for dancing (and her classes in Manhattan) and turn to something more practical that would insure her financial future. According to Jennifer, "Where I come from, you got a job as a bank teller and got married, and being driven [professionally] didn't mean wanting to be a star. It meant being a lawyer instead of a secretary."

Jennifer, who had worked in a lawyer's office in her part-time job, thought that studying to be a lawyer seemed dull compared to her show business aspirations. Later, looking back on this career option, Jennifer would joke, "Actually, I think I would have been an OK lawyer. I don't think I would have been a very happy lawyer. I would be in front of the jury, singing."

3

STEPPING OUT INTO THE WORLD

Jennifer graduated from Preston High School in 1987 and then enrolled at Baruch College in Manhattan, mainly to appease her determined parents. Jennifer dutifully began her studies at Baruch, but her heart was not in them. After one semester, she dropped out, which upset her parents. She says, "They thought it was really stupid to go off and try to be a movie star. No Latinas did that—it was just this stupid, foolish . . . idea to my parents and to everybody who knew me."

These differences over Jennifer's future led to a big fight between Jennifer and her parents. Eventually, she moved out on her own, living with various new acquaintances in Manhattan, often sharing a tiny apartment with three or four other roommates. For a while she continued with her part-time job at the Bronx law firm. The job helped to pay her modest living expenses, for her ballet and jazz dance classes, and for visits to local dance clubs to hear the latest music and see the newest dance steps being performed.

While Jennifer had the ongoing encouragement of her boyfriend David Cruz—to whom she became engaged—it hurt her to be at such odds with her parents. However, she could not go along with their less risky plan for her future. While she disagreed with their viewpoint, she understood the reasons for her parents' approach, in which "there was as much a fear of success as a fear of failure."

Despite the uncertainty of her future, 18-year-old Jennifer had a strong sense of self and was confident in her ambition of becoming a professional dancer and actor. Always spirited, her rule of thumb was and still is, "You have to believe in yourself. If you don't, nobody will. So I believed—no matter how many times I cried myself to sleep or ate another slice of pizza [as her daily big meal]."

With faith in herself, Jennifer doggedly pursued her own course, refusing to be discouraged by the slim chance of succeeding in show business.

Paying Her Dues

On her own in Manhattan, Jennifer endured the typical struggles of an aspiring professional dancer. "There were times when I was really down to my last dollar. And then my last fifty cents . . . and then my last quarter." Despite the tough times, she refused to abandon her career vision. She auditioned for the chorus of Broadway musicals, but had no success. She did find acceptance in the then new world of music videos, which had been popularized by such cable networks as MTV and VH1. Jennifer recalls, "I'd dance in [a Manhattan club to] a piece-of-garbage rap or pop video for 50 bucks and make the money last a whole month." With her energetic, slick dance moves, Jennifer found recurrent work at such Manhattan dance forums as the Cat Club. Not only did such assignments pay the bills, but it gave the dedicated dancer opportunities and motivation to improve her dance steps.

What really turned matters around professionally for Jennifer was the success of rap artist MC Hammer in the late 1980s. The flamboyant performer is credited with being the first key artist to bring rap music to the attention of a large pop music audience. With such hit singles as Hammer's "U Can't Touch This," which won two Grammy Awards, hip-hop went mainstream. According to Jennifer, "All the auditions started becoming hip-hop auditions. I was good at it, and they were like, 'Ooh, a light-skinned girl who can do that. Great, let's hire her!" Jennifer began to frequently find work in music videos.

The success of recording artists such as MC Hammer (pictured above) brought rap to a mainstream audience. This created many job opportunities for Jennifer, who was skilled at dancing to hip-hop music and appeared in several music videos. (Photofest)

During this period Jennifer also performed in regional productions of the musicals *Jesus Christ, Superstar* and *Oklahoma!* Her persistence paid off when she won a chorus part in *Golden Musicals of Broadway*, a revue that toured Europe for five months. While most everyone else in the production eventually got to perform solos in the show, Jennifer did not, and she felt slighted. Feeling depressed, she called her mother to complain. Jennifer recalls, "I thought she'd offer me some sympathy. Instead, she said, 'Don't you ever call me crying again. You wanted to be in this business, so you better toughen up!'" It was a lesson in tough love. It had its intended positive effect on Jennifer, no matter how much it hurt Lupe to be stern with her fledgling performer daughter.

Jennifer went abroad again, this time as part of the show *Synchronicity*. For this musical, which played in Japan, she acted as a dancer, singer, and choreographer. From her appearances in such shows—and from auditioning for other parts that she did not win—Jennifer developed a survival attitude: "If you're gonna make it in this business, you need the kind of personality that you have to do it or die, there's no alternative."

In staying afloat in the show business game, Jennifer not only relied on her talent and determination, but also on her ability to meet new challenges head on. For example, one day she auditioned for a TV commercial to promote the upcoming Olympics. The director asked if she knew how to use a trampoline. Although she did not, she replied, "Yeah, of course." As time went on, Jennifer learned that performing in commercials was generally not for her. "I had to give up doing them because I just couldn't do them convincingly. I have to believe in what I'm doing."

Hollywood Beckons

In April 1990, the Fox TV network had debuted the half-hour comedy/variety show called *In Living Color*. The show was created by Keenen Ivory Wayans, who functioned as the program's producer, writer, actor, and performer. The show was regarded as a mostly African-American version of the long-running *Saturday Night Live*. The cast featured several of Keenen's siblings, as well as such other cast regulars as Jim Carrey, Tommy Davidson, and David Alan Grier. One of the show's recurring features was the Fly Girls. This energetic troupe of five dancers backed up guest musical acts, participated in the background of some sketches, and had occasional featured dance spots on the fast-paced proceedings.

After a few successful months on air, *In Living Color* was renewed for the fall season. By then one of the regular Fly Girls was unavailable to continue with the show. This led dancer/actor Rosie Perez, who was the show's choreographer, to conduct nationwide auditions for a replacement. The network put out casting calls that drew over 2,000 applicants to test for the coveted spot.

One of those who tried out was Jennifer. She made it to the finals, but another contestant won the heated competition. Then, suddenly, the winner was unable to accept the job, and Jennifer, the runner-up, was asked to join *In Living Color*.

Although she was thrilled by an offer that would put her on national TV, Jennifer was initially hesitant in taking the assignment because it meant relocating to the West Coast. However, when her boyfriend, David Cruz, agreed to relocate to Los Angeles to be with Jennifer, she said yes. According to Lopez, joining *In Living Color* "brought me to Los Angeles, and it put me in the center of the business. I saw the way in [to the entertainment business] at that point."

In comparison to the rest of the Fly Girls, Jennifer was not thin or refined in her looks. Rosie Perez, a Puerto Rican–American like Jennifer, said later about having hired Lopez: "She wasn't the great dancer. The other Fly Girls had more talent and experience, but she had a look that I knew the audience would tune in to." Jennifer felt like the odd person out in the dance troupe, a situation not helped by the occasional clashes of temperament she had with Perez. Several of the Fly Girls taunted the newcomer about her voluptuous figure and her very New York look and speech. When Jennifer mentioned the situation to Keenen Ivory Wayans, he told Jennifer, "Success is the best revenge."

Determined to succeed in spite of the obstacles, Jennifer soon adjusted her dance movements to meet the show's demands. Before long, Jennifer found that she could handle her routines at *In Living Color*. Feeling more confident, she soon began to enjoy her weekly TV outing. In coping with her work challenges and dealing with living so far from home, Jennifer was greatly comforted when David Cruz arrived in L.A. to be with her full time. As Lopez points out, "I was stable at home, so I was able to excel and work."

Hungry for the Spotlight

As one TV season passed into the next, Jennifer began to feel limited by her dance chorus role on *In Living Color*. To fill her spare time when she was not with David, she took acting classes. Increasingly restless because she no longer felt challenged by her role on *In Living Color*, she again conferred with Keenen Ivory Wayans. He advised her to stay with the program to gain further experience and industry exposure and then move on to other show business opportunities. Jennifer agreed.

Meanwhile, in 1991 Jennifer had become friendly with Eric Gold, a member of the TV show's production team.

They exchanged confidences about their career dreams. The next year, when Eric Gold branched out into talent management, he became manager for both Jennifer and fellow *In Living Color* cast member Jim Carrey. A key reason that Gold gambled on Lopez's potential was, "There was just an unshakable confidence about Jennifer. No doubt, no fear. The girl just had it."

It was Gold who advised Jennifer that if she wanted to make the transition from dancer to actor she must lose weight and tone up her body. Immediately heeding this advice, Jennifer began working with a trainer and started jogging to get in better physical shape. Explaining her decision she said, "I knew how important it was for me to look good. I was a Latina actress. I didn't want to be relegated to being given 'the maid' or 'the mistress' roles for the rest of my life. Really, I had to look better than good if I wanted to be noticed." As part of her strict regimen, Jennifer consulted with a dietitian from whom she learned to balance her intake of carbohydrates, fats, and protein, and to cut down on her portions.

With her new sleek figure, 5'6", Jennifer found outside employment dancing in music videos. She was one of the dancers in Janet Jackson's 1993 video "That's the Way Love Goes." Such professional exposure, along with Lopez's recurring participation on *In Living Color*, gave her increased standing in the show business community.

By now, several of the original *In Living Color* cast members—including Keenen Ivory and Damon Wayans—had left the TV series as a result of a dispute with upper management at the Fox network. Others in the remaining crew were looking for ways to turn their current weekly TV jobs into new gigs.

During a seasonal break from *In Living Color*, Jennifer was cast in a CBS TV movie *Nurses on the Line: The Crash of Flight 7*. The film dealt with student nurses, doctors, and other passengers aboard a plane that crashes in the Mexican jungle. Jennifer was cast as Rosie Romero, one of the young nurses. She was not proud of this made-for-television film, but she wanted to expand her show business resume to include acting assignments.

During 1993 there was talk of spinning off the well-liked Fly Girls into their own weekly TV vehicle. One of those approached to guide such a property was veteran TV writer/producer Ralph Farquhar. He was brought to the studio set to meet with the Fly Girls to see if it sparked ideas on how best to showcase them. Farquhar quickly decided that this potential venture was not for him. However, before he left the sound stage that day, he was approached by Jennifer. At that time, she had made a point of keeping up with new TV and film ideas in Hollywood. She knew that Fahrquhar was involved with a pending TV series that was to shoot a pilot episode. She

asked him (and his collaborator Michael Weithorn) to consider her for a part in this project, *South Central*, a com-
edy/drama set in Los Angeles.

To Jennifer's great satisfaction, Farquhar later got back
in touch with her and included her in *South Central*. When
the entry was being shopped around to the TV networks,
Jeff Sagansky, then the president of CBS-TV, saw footage
of the entry that included a brief on-camera appearance
by Jennifer. Sagansky recalls, "I think she had one line,
maybe two. I turned to the person who was in charge of
our casting and said after that one line, 'Sign that girl.
She's a star.' It was that clear."

Moving Ahead

While the makers of *South Central* were looking for a network
for their show, Jennifer joined the cast of a new TV serial
drama called *Second Chances*. The one-hour CBS network
show starred Connie Sellecca as a lawyer whose husband is
murdered. Among the several story lines in this nighttime
soap opera was a plot thread involving Melinda Lopez
(played by Jennifer), a Mexican-American student who must
cope with an overly protective father. She also has to deal
with her problematic marriage to a blueblood law student
who comes from a socially prominent, snobbish family.

Second Chances premiered in December 1993 with a
two-hour pilot episode that generated good ratings and

earned critical praise. Although the show trailed behind its competition on the Thursday night schedule, CBS stood by their new entry. However, fate intervened. First it became known that star Connie Sellecca had become pregnant, which would limit her availability for future episodes. Then in mid-January 1994, southern California suffered a severe earthquake. In its wake, the sets on the *Second Chances* sound stages were extensively damaged. Efforts to salvage even a portion of the expensive scenery proved too costly, and the series abruptly ended.

Thereafter, CBS-TV asked the *Second Chances* producers to come up with a new serial drama that would premiere as a summer series. They created *Hotel Malibu*, which revolved around the Mayfield family, who operate the Hotel Malibu on the scenic southern California coast. CBS and the producers decided to carry over the characters of Melinda Lopez and her father from *Second Chances.*

Hotel Malibu premiered on August 4, 1994. But with disappointing ratings, the show vanished after its September 8, 1994 episode aired.

Meanwhile, on April 5, 1994, previously shot episodes of *South Central* finally were seen on the Fox TV network. The show revolved around a divorced African-American woman struggling to raise her family in a difficult inner-city neighborhood of Los Angeles. The lead role of Joan Mosley was handled by Tina Lifford. At the local food coop where Joan works, other employees include Jennifer Lopez's character Lucille.

In her limited acting assignment on this summer TV series, Jennifer registered well. She displayed naturalness and an appealing vitality that matched her new look. While many TV viewers and critics were appreciative of *South Central*'s mature writing and three-dimensional characters, other watchers found the show too gritty and depressing (even with the program's frequent use of comic relief). By the end of August 1994, when the show's rating had not improved, Fox cancelled the program.

Now the veteran of four TV series, Jennifer was ready to move on to fresh career challenges. In the prior four years she had demonstrated an increased versatility on camera, an essential ingredient for her professional growth. Far more seasoned and polished as a performer than when she had come to Los Angeles in 1994, ambitious Jennifer now had her sights set on making feature films and proving her potential in that challenging medium.

4

THE ROAD TO MOVIE FAME

Distinguished filmmaker Gregory Nava celebrates his Latin-American roots in much of his big- and small-screen work. His 1983 film *El Norte* was the story of a brother and sister in Guatemala who survive a massacre in their Mayan peasant village. Thereafter, they make the perilous trek north, hoping for a better life in the United States. The emotional film was nominated for an Academy Award for its powerful screenplay, which was written by Nava and his wife, Anna Thomas.

A decade later Nava and Thomas collaborated on the script to *My Family/Mi Familia* (1995). The new project concerned three generations of a Mexican-American family as seen through the eyes of a family member (played by Edward James Olmos), who is a writer. The touching story focuses on the dramatic life of the head of the family, Jose Sanchez. Back in the early 1920s, when he is a teenager,

Jose leaves his remote Mexican village and comes across the U.S. border to settle in Los Angeles. There he becomes a gardener and, while working in Beverly Hills, meets a housekeeper, Maria. By the 1930s the couple is married and has two children. While she is pregnant with a third child, Maria is caught in a sweep by U.S. immigration officials. Although she is an American citizen, she is deported to Mexico. It takes two years for Maria (and her baby son) to make the hazardous journey back to East L.A. to be reunited with her family. The film, full of laughter and tears, follows the fate of the generations of Sanchez children as they struggle to be regarded as real Americans while not abandoning their Mexican heritage.

Jennifer auditioned for and won the role of the young Maria in *My Family/Mi Familia*. She had several touching scenes in the film. In one, she grasps her infant son as she crosses a river to make her way back to her loved ones in Los Angeles. *My Family/Mi Familia* was released in May 1995 and received much critical praise.

Despite Jennifer's limited amount of screen time in the film, she made a strong impression on both filmgoers and professionals within the movie industry. Nava publicly complimented Jennifer for being "beautiful and phenomenally gifted." For her performance in the film, Jennifer was nominated for a best supporting actress Independent Spirit Award.

Jennifer and actor Jacob Vargas in My Family/Mi Familia. *Jennifer received praise for her supporting role in this film.* (Photofest)

Building Her Image

Eager to continue the career momentum she gained with *My Family/Mi Familia*, Jennifer accepted a tempting offer to appear in *Money Train* (1995), a big-budget action feature from a major studio (Columbia Pictures). The film stars Wesley Snipes and Woody Harrelson as foster brothers employed as undercover New York City transit cops. The duo's new partner, a rookie named Grace Santiago, quickly becomes the object of affection for both men.

The *Money Train* producers had been searching for a leading lady who could play a feisty New Yorker, tackle the demanding physical aspects of the role, and handle the film's interracial-romance theme. As a physically fit Puerto Rican–American who grew up in the Bronx, Jennifer was a natural fit for the role of Grace. Having beaten out many other applicants for the part, she received a salary of $200,000 to appear in *Money Train*. It was four times what she had earned for *My Family/Mi Familia*. Although the film wasn't a big hit with viewers or critics, it helped Jennifer gain notoriety in Hollywood.

Changing Relationships

While shooting *Money Train,* Jennifer deflected unwanted off-camera romantic attention from both Wesley Snipes and Woody Harrelson. She politely explained to each actor that she was involved in a long-term romantic relationship with David Cruz and was not interested in their advances.

Having survived the on- and off-camera obstacles of making *Money Train*, Jennifer returned to her life in Los Angeles. She discovered, however, that the situation had changed with her boyfriend, David. Her career success was quickly escalating, which created new demands and pressures for her. It left little time for a satisfactory home life. Moreover, David was finding it difficult to establish a living for himself in Los Angeles. More and more he felt out of place in his relationship with his increasingly high-profile girlfriend. After much discussion, the couple regretfully decided to separate. Cruz returned to the Bronx where he opened a dry-cleaning business. Jennifer commented later, "Career-wise, we weren't in the same place. He just didn't know what he wanted to do. . . . I was so fast. I was like a rocket, he was like a rock."

Putting aside her feelings about the breakup, Jennifer returned to work. Her next screen assignment was in a film called *Jack* (1996). The movie was produced and directed by Francis Ford Coppola, acclaimed as the filmmaker of *The Godfather* (1972) and *Apocalypse Now* (1979), and starred Robin Williams. Coppola's American Zoetrope Company had been a producer of *My Family/Mi Familia*. When he saw a screening of that picture, he turned to director Gregory Nava and asked who the beautiful woman was who had played the young Maria. Francis learned the performer was Jennifer Lopez, and he was determined to use her in a film project one day soon.

Coppola had the opportunity to hire Jennifer after she auditioned for a featured role in *Jack*. As would occur so frequently for Jennifer in her career, she came across very well at auditions and won the acting assignment. (In discussing her success at auditions, Jennifer explains, "People just seem to respond to me when I go in to read for them." She further explains, "A lot of people go into meetings and auditions all nervous. No! You've got to have 'wow!' I tell my actress friends this all the time. I walk into auditions going, 'What's gonna make me different from all the other girls here?' They're looking for the next star to walk into that room. It's about being alive, open, electric, confident. That's the 'wow.'")

Jack is comedy/drama about a 10-year-old boy who suffers from a rare genetic disease that causes him to age at four times the normal rate. His concerned parents keep him sheltered at home, fearing that he will be scorned by the other students if he goes to school. However, because their boy is so lonely, they eventually agree that he can enroll in the fifth grade. There he deals with the mixed reactions of his classmates and quickly develops a crush on his beautiful, caring teacher, Miss Marquez, played by Jennifer.

Jennifer readily accepted this acting assignment for several reasons. She very much wanted the opportunity to work with both Francis Ford Coppola and Robin Williams. In addition, she was drawn to the picture because her role was not ethnic-specific. She felt parts such as this would help her gain mainstream acceptance with moviemakers and with filmgoers. Then too, she was excited by the part she would play. "My character is kind of [Jack's] saving grace. She's there for him when he's lonely and makes sure the other kids don't pick on him. What's most fasci-

Robin Williams and Jennifer in Jack (Photofest)

nating to my character, Miss Marquez, is how normal Jack looks. But when you look into his eyes, you can tell he's a boy." She further pointed out, "The tragedy of Jack's life is that he probably will never have a romantic relationship. Miss Marquez realizes that, and it breaks her heart. It's a heartbreaking story. Jack is cheated out of a lot of things that we all get to experience in life—the joys of life."

In preparing for *Jack*, Coppola arranged for the cast to spend two weeks at his home in scenic Napa Valley, California. There the actors (including Jennifer, Robin Williams, and Bill Cosby, among others) became acquainted with one another and delved into the script. Although such an outing is not a standard part of making a movie, Jennifer said, "It was an incredible experience. . . . We got to know each other as our characters. It was a process I hadn't been through with any other director. I taught class to the boys. They'd get out of hand, the way that boys do, but it went well. And they taught me a thing or two." She also admitted about her stay at the Coppolas': "I'm a city girl, and there must have been too much clean air or something, because I got a little ill."

During the actual shooting of *Jack* in San Francisco, Jennifer got along well with both crew and cast. She especially enjoyed working with the energetic Robin Williams both on and off camera. Says Jennifer, "In between scenes he'd want to play, so we'd do things like *Romeo and Juliet* as performed by Sylvester Stallone and Rosie Perez."

Despite everyone's high expectations for *Jack*, the picture failed to stir great enthusiasm when released in August 1996. Janet Maslin (*New York Times*) criticized the story as predictable. Roger Ebert (*Chicago Sun-Times*) felt the movie did not come together satisfactorily. However, he wrote, "There is one scene that works, is true, and does illuminate Jack's human dilemma. That's the scene where he gets a crush on his teacher (Jennifer Lopez) and plies her with a bag of red Gummi Bears before asking her to the school dance. (She's the only female in view who is tall enough to dance with him.) The way the teacher tactfully and gently handles this situation is an illustration of a path the whole movie could have taken, had it been more ambitious."

Although Jennifer had relatively few scenes in *Jack* compared to star Robin Williams, she was acclaimed for her gorgeous looks on camera and for her display of increasingly fine acting skills. For her work in *Jack* (as well as *Money Train*), Lopez was nominated for an NCRL Bravo trophy by the National Council of La Raza, the nation's largest Hispanic civil rights organization. The trophy honors actors and directors who promote positive portrayals of Hispanics in the media.

Building on Success and Finding a New Love

While promoting *Money Train* in late 1995, Jennifer told the media, "God is watching over me, that's all I can say. He has a plan for me. I've been really lucky. And I work hard."

Publicity-wise Jennifer was gaining prominence both within the film industry and in the public spotlight. Increasingly her interviews and photos appeared in the media. Also during this period, she had the honor of being selected as the cover model for the premier issue of *Latina*, a new magazine for Hispanic women.

Meanwhile, being increasingly in demand for Hollywood projects, Jennifer was cast in *Blood and Wine* (1996), a crime thriller directed by Bob Rafelson and starring Jack Nicholson. Both Rafelson and Nicholson were known for being exacting, unconventional, and risk-taking in their careers. Jennifer was somewhat intimidated by this big-screen project in which she would play Gabriela, the Cuban maid who is the mistress of Nicholson's character.

Blood and Wine falls within the film noir tradition, where people are victims to their worst impulses and usu-ally suffer tragic fates. The downbeat story concerns a Miami wine merchant (Nicholson) who teams with a slick, ailing safecracker (played by Michael Caine) to heist a $1 million necklace. Complicating matters, Nicholson's character is coping with the ruins of his marriage, handling a resentful stepson, and trying to keep his stunning mistress (Lopez) from double-crossing him.

Jennifer recalls of the film, "I remember the first day of rehearsal. He [Nicholson] came in, sat down and the director wanted me to sit next to him because ours was the prominent man-woman relationship in the film. Michael Caine was sitting on the other side, and I looked at one and then the other. Then it was like I had an out-of-body experience! I wondered to myself: 'What am I doing in this room with these people?' It was very scary. But fun." Keeping her concerns to herself, Jennifer regained her composure by telling herself, "OK. I'm here for a reason. I'm here because they think I can do this. So if they think I can do it, I think I can do it."

Initially there were supposed to be very physically revealing scenes between Jennifer's character and Jack's. However, as the film proceeded, the love scenes were toned down. Nevertheless, the on-screen love sequences proved a big challenge to Jennifer. She has said, "That's the only time I've ever thought about quitting [a project]. I had grown up very traditional, Catholic. I was like, 'I don't like this.'" However, veteran Nicholson came to her rescue. According to Jennifer, "He saw that I was getting a little jazzed. Y'know, too much going on. He told me it's all about controlling that. Then he said, "This is just about us.' It really helped."

By the time *Blood and Wine* finished production, Jennifer felt far more confident of her abilities to hold her own against formidable actors such as Nicholson and Caine. She was also pleased that during one sequence—which called for Jack and her to perform a steamy salsa dance—it was she who had to instruct her Oscar-winning co-lead in the finer points of the dance.

While her movie career was reaching new heights, Jennifer had also found a new real-life romance. His name was Ojani Noa, a young Cuban refugee who worked at a trendy restaurant in Miami Beach. What started out as a spontaneous infatuation between Lopez and Noa would soon develop into a full-blown relationship.

5

REACHING
FOR THE TOP

Reportedly, when Jennifer Lopez first saw Ojani Noa waiting on tables at the Larios restaurant in Miami Beach, she told her assistant, "That's the man I'm going to marry." However, the couple first had to actually meet. Shy about being the aggressor in a potential love match, Jennifer also was not fluent in Spanish, which, she had learned, was Ojani's first language.

Eventually, however, after Jennifer returned to the restaurant several times and made sure to often walk by Ojani's workstation, the couple exchanged a few words. On another occasion at Larios, thanks to Jennifer's matchmaking assistant, Lopez was seated at one of Ojani's tables. One thing led to another, and the duo's romance quickly blossomed. As the couple got to know each other, Jennifer learned that in 1992 Ojani had escaped from Cuba on a raft and made the perilous trek to Miami through shark-infested waters. The handsome young man had ambitions of becoming a model and, perhaps, an actor.

Although Lopez was very excited about her new boyfriend, she had to temporarily leave him to go on location to make her next picture. In high demand professionally, Jennifer had been offered the choice of two upcoming Columbia Pictures projects: a romantic comedy (*Fools Rush In*) or a horror thriller (*Anaconda*). She decided the former was too lightweight and rejected that work option. Instead, Jennifer, already a tough negotiator in the Hollywood business, agreed for a $1 million fee to track through the dangerous wilds of Brazil to shoot *Anaconda*, a project that she labeled a "fun B-movie." She was excited by the challenge of taking on such an athletic leading role in an action picture and picking a part that was not geared to any specific ethnic type. It was the kind of action lead that Hollywood usually reserved for male stars like Bruce Willis. In casting Jennifer for this focal assignment, Peruvian-born director Luis Losa observed, "She's sweet, sensual, but also has an inner dignity."

Anaconda is about an anthropologist (played by Eric Stoltz) who joins a documentary filmmaker (Jennifer) on an expedition in search of a long-lost native tribe. Along their way through the Brazilian rain forest, they are joined by a crazed hunter (portrayed by Jon Voight), set on capturing a legendary, 40-foot-long anaconda. The reptile-infested odyssey proves a deadly nightmare. The heroine and her ace cameraman (played by rapper Ice Cube) are among the plot's few survivors.

Anxious to prove herself as a willing, able performer, Jennifer did not hesitate to undertake the tough physical activity required for *Anaconda*. In fact, Jennifer thrived on such treacherous work. Making the difficult location shoot in Brazil far more enjoyable was the fact that Ojani Noa was hired on as Jennifer's personal trainer.

With its clichéd plot and animatronic monster snake, it was impossible for most critics to take *Anaconda* seriously. However, the film's mixture of thrills and camp proved excellent fare for action-hungry audiences. The movie made $135.6 million in worldwide distribution. As a result, in Hollywood's terms, Jennifer Lopez was now a fast-rising movie personality who could open a picture well and help to insure the screen project's financial success at the box office.

A Defining Role

On March 31, 1995, at a motel in Corpus Christi, Texas, the famed Latina singer Selena Pérez was fatally shot by Yolanda Saldivar, the former president of Selena's fan club and the manager of her boutique in San Antonio. The death of Selena, at age 23, caused tremendous grief within the Latino community. A beloved figure in North America to both young and old, this spirited young singer was known especially for performing songs in the Tejano style. (Tejano is a type of Tex-Mex pop music that features the accordion and blends the polka with assorted forms of traditional Mexican music. More recently, synthesizers and other rock instruments have become part of the Tejano mix.)

Selena was born to Mexican-American parents in April 1971 in Lake Jackson, Texas. Her dad, Abraham Quintanilla Jr., had once been a musician, part of the group known as Los Dinos. By age 10, Selena began performing with her father as her manager and Los Dinos as her onstage band. In 1983, she made her recording debut. (English was Selena's first language, although she grew up understanding Spanish. Her initial work was recorded in Spanish with Selena singing the words phonetically. After her music began to gain popularity, she took lessons to learn Spanish. By the time of her murder, she was fluent in the language.)

In 1987, at the Tejano Music Awards, Selena was selected both Female Vocalist of the Year and Performer of the Year. Two years later she signed with EMI's Latin division and soon released her first album (*Selena*). The title track from her next release (*Ven Conmigo*) was the first

The Tejano music star Selena, whose successful career was cut short by her murder in 1995 (Photofest)

Tejano record to go gold (in other words, it sold more than 500,000 copies).

In April 1992 Selena married Chris Pérez, the lead guitarist of Los Dinos. The next year the rising young singer earned her first Grammy for her album *Selena Live* in the category of Best Mexican American Performance. That same year, the hardworking singer released an album of love songs (*Quiero*) and made her film debut in *Don Juan DeMarco*, a picture costarring Johnny Depp and Marlon Brando.

In this same period, Selena, long noted for her colorful and sexy onstage outfits, began a clothing manufacturing business. In addition, the title cut from her 1994 album, *Amor Prohibido*, won a Grammy and went gold. During the spring of 1995, Selena, already a millionaire, recorded her first English-language album (*Dreaming of You*). It was then that she had the fateful encounter with Saldivar. (In November 1995, Saldivar, who still claimed to be innocent, was convicted of killing Selena and sentenced to a minimum of 30 years in prison.)

Selena's crossover album, *Dreaming of You*, was released after her death, in the summer of 1995. It became the first Tejano album to reach number one in America, and more than 2 million copies were sold by the year's end.

In the wake of Selena's tragic death, several movie producers were considering making a screen biography of the late singer. Rather than lose control over the retelling of his daughter's life, Abraham Quintanilla sought professional advice as to who should write and direct the movie biography. Quintanilla was told that Gregory Nava was the right match for the project. The two men met and came to an agreement which led to Warner Bros. producing the nearly $20 million film project.

From the start of casting *Selena* (1997), finding the right talent for the title role was crucial. There was the usual debate about whether to hire an unknown or a known actress for the pivotal assignment. A massive talent hunt was conducted across the United States. Many thousands of applicants were anxious to be auditioned for the picture.

Knowing that Nava was in charge of the project and that he had appreciated her screen work in *My Family/Mi Familia,* Jennifer hoped that he might consider her to play the late singer. Sure enough, she was asked to try out for the movie. During her audition Jennifer read aloud several script pages and performed nine minutes of singing/dancing. As usual, she made an impressive presentation for the decision-makers. By now she had learned the key to such make-or-break career situations: "There's no way you can put a character together for an audition. But you can give the idea of whether you have the required charisma and the ability to do it." Wisely she did not allow herself to be concerned that she was competing against unknowns for this important job. In due time, Jennifer was notified that the part and a $1 million salary were hers.

Becoming Selena

When Jennifer was announced as the final choice to star in *Selena,* there was an outcry from some displeased fans that a Puerto Rican–American should not be portraying the famous Mexican-American. Putting aside such concerns, Jennifer became more and more enthusiastic about the upcoming project. She was thrilled to be playing the late singer on-screen. She emotionally connected to the real-life Selena because the singer "embraced the fact that she was Latina and showed the world that there is beauty in diversity."

To thoroughly research her upcoming role, Jennifer watched videos of Selena, listened to her albums, and met with individuals who had known the famed vocalist. As her intense preparation continued, Lopez realized there were many similarities between herself and her movie character. "We were approximately the same age, we had the same kind of career, and we were both becoming successful. She was very close with her family, as I am. She was with one guy, and I was with one guy too, for most of my life. So, there was a lot with which I identified, plus everything I learned."

To further understand her film alter ego, Jennifer spent time living in the Quintanilla household, going through family albums, talking with relatives, and absorbing the personalities of the people key to Selena's life: her parents, siblings, and husband. At Mr. Quintanilla's insistence, it was agreed that Selena's singing would be used in the film and that Jennifer would lip-synch the words to these songs. However, during the large concert sequences, it was decided that Lopez would actually sing (although her voice cannot be heard on the film's soundtrack) so that it would not be obvious that she was lip-synching for the cameras.

Another aspect of preparing for the movie musical was to test various makeup (including a prosthetic nose) to see how close Jennifer could come to resembling Selena without taking away from her own look. Eventually, the nose was discarded as were plans to have Lopez's golden hazel eyes transformed to dark brown (the color of Selena's) with tinted contact lenses. Through a combination of makeup and tanning booth sessions, Jennifer's skin was deepened to approximate that of Selena's.

Rounding out the main cast for this screen biography were Edward James Olmos and Constance Marie (both from *My Family/Mi Familia*) as the parents; Jon Seda as Selena's husband; Jacob Vargas and Jackie Guerra as the siblings; and Lupe Ontiveros as Yolanda Saldivar. Filming began in the late summer of 1996 in San Antonio, Texas, with further location work in other parts of Texas, Mexico, and Los Angeles.

In one of those magical transformations that sometimes occur in memorable filmmaking, Jennifer "became" Selena. Jennifer said later, "Selena was there with me all through the filming. It was just a matter of feeling confident enough to let go of myself and allow Selena to take over. It was her spirit that was with me. It was a great feeling for me."

Wanting her parents to experience some of the excitement of the film project, Jennifer had them fly to San Antonio to be at the Alamodome (substituting in the picture for the Houston Astrodome) where Lopez would film important scenes recreating the singing star's last public concert, given just weeks before her murder. Nervous about performing in front of a crowd of more than 30,000 extras, Jennifer wondered if the audience—many of them diehard Selena fans—would accept her as their beloved idol. When Jennifer stepped on stage, she looked and moved very much like the late vocalist. The crowd went wild, some shouting, "Selena!" and others yelling, "Jennifer!" Then and there, the moviemakers realized that they didn't have to worry about the public reacting negatively to Jennifer's interpretation of the role.

Thrilled by the audience's reaction and sparked by her inner excitement at performing live on stage for a big audience, Jennifer said, "There's nothing like singing in front of an audience." After the completion of that emotional sequence, she rushed to phone her agent in Los Angeles and told him, "I gotta record something."

Good Times Ahead

When *Selena* finished shooting, there was the typical wrap party for cast and crew. One surprising turn at the celebration was when Ojani Noa stood front and center, got down on bended knee, pulled out an engagement ring, and asked Jennifer to marry him. With great surprise and joy, she said yes.

Selena debuted on March 21, 1997. Critic Roger Ebert (*Chicago Sun-Times*) was strongly impressed by this musical biography, especially because "It's insightful in portraying Mexican-American culture as a rich resource with its own flavor and character." As for Lopez, Ebert regarded this as a "star-making performance." He reasoned, "After her strong work as the passionate lover of Jack Nicholson in the current *Blood and Wine*, here she creates a completely different performance, as a loyal Quintanilla who does most of her growing up on a tour bus with her dad at the wheel." Jack Matthews (*Newsday*) noted that in the film's final montage, there were shots "of the real Selena in performance, underscoring the brilliance of Lopez's performance."

Rolling Stone praised the film, saying, "Jennifer Lopez excels as Selena. . . ."

Even though it was not especially geared to a mainstream American audience, *Selena* did well in U.S. theaters. Jennifer's performance proved that she could not be only extremely appealing on camera, but that she also had the dramatic range to carry such a strong story. For her performance in *Selena*, Jennifer was nominated for, among other prizes, a Golden Globe Award for best actress. She won an Alma Award for best actress, presented by the NCLR, for her work in *Selena* as well as for her participation in *Anaconda*. (In Spanish, the word *alma* means *soul* or *spirit*.)

Reviewing her show business career to date, Jennifer had every right to be highly satisfied with her progress within the entertainment industry. However, she observed to *Time* magazine in 1997, "I'm fortunate because I've built up a little body of work. Still, there aren't a lot of parts for us [Latinas], and we're not generally considered for other roles that aren't race specific. It's

Jennifer Lopez, as Selena, sings for a crowd in the film Selena. *Jennifer's highly praised work in the film inspired her to pursue a recording career.* (Photofest)

starting to change a little bit, but we're still treated like foreigners who just got here because we're not white. But we're as American as they come!"

6

THE NEW SUPERSTAR

On Saturday, February 22, 1997—just after *Blood and Wine* had quietly opened in the United States and weeks before *Selena* and *Anaconda* would be issued—Jennifer wed Ojani Noa in Miami. After mingling with the 200 guests (which included Jennifer's family, Ojani's relatives who lived in the area, film directors Gregory Nava and Oliver Stone, and actor Edward James Olmos), the newlyweds phoned Ojani's parents in Cuba. Then the couple set out in the groom's truck for a weeklong honeymoon in Key West, Florida.

For Jennifer, such a "long" stretch of professional inactivity was most unusual at this stage of her nonstop career. In the prior several months, she had made four feature films back to back. The last of this quartet had been Oliver Stone's *U-Turn* (1997) for TriStar Pictures. When the director was casting the crime drama (at the time Jennifer was preparing to go to Brazil to make *Anaconda*), he had requested a meeting with Lopez, but she had refused. Her rationale was that three years prior, when Stone had been planning a picture (which was never made), Jennifer had tested with the filmmaker for a part in the project. In the midst of her audition, Stone began busying himself with rearranging the furniture, papers, and so forth in his office. Jennifer had been stunned by this apparent rudeness. Later, still smarting from the slight, she angrily told her agent that she would never again audition for the noted moviemaker.

When Jennifer showed no interest in being cast in *U-Turn*, Stone contacted her directly and persuaded her to meet with him. She finally agreed to the conference, where she read for the role of the femme fatale. Her character (Grace McKenna) was a sultry Apache Native American who lives in a small southwestern town near the desert. She becomes romantically involved with a recently arrived small-time hoodlum (to be played by Sean Penn). Soon she convinces the newcomer to murder her loutish husband (to be portrayed by Nick Nolte). Meanwhile the drifter has been asked by the spouse to kill his unfaithful wife.

Stone was impressed with Jennifer and soon assured her that the role would be hers. Time passed and Jennifer learned that movie star Sharon Stone was now interested

Jennifer and Ojani Noa (Landov)

in playing Grace McKenna in *U-Turn*. Jennifer assumed that her better-known rival would get the part. However, Oliver ultimately offered the part to Jennifer. For a $1 million fee, she accepted the deal.

Jennifer found director Stone to be both charming and accommodating to her on the set. Although she had agreed to a nude scene within the film, she still hoped it might not come to pass. (She explained, "Jennifer the actress has nothing against nudity, but Jennifer the person really hates it. The actress always wins out by reminding me this is what I'm paid to do.")

Made on a relatively low $20 million budget, *U-Turn* was shot in 42 days with location work in Arizona and Nevada. Jennifer and co-lead Sean Penn got along extremely well on the shoot.

Despite the creative effort put into *U-Turn*, it failed to entice critics or filmgoers.

Moving into the Big League

George Clooney had enjoyed a huge career boost by playing the womanizing pediatrician Dr. Douglas Ross on the hit TV series *ER,* which debuted in 1995. Since then he had alternated between starring on his TV show and making theatrical releases (for example, 1996's *One Fine Day* and 1997's *Batman & Robin*). However, he had not yet experienced a major box-office success. He now had high hopes for an upcoming project, *Out of Sight,* a crime drama filled with romance and comedy. The plot centered on a bank robber who breaks out of prison and then becomes romantically involved with a female U.S. marshal whom he has kidnapped.

Clooney and his management wanted him to have proper on-screen chemistry with his leading lady—something lacking in his recent big-screen entries. For a while, Sandra Bullock was favored for the role of Karen Sisco, the U.S. marshal. However, Bullock reportedly refused to screen test for the part. Clooney insisted that the actor playing the role of the female lawmaker must audition to confirm that he and she would make an appealing screen team.

Unlike the more firmly established Bullock, Jennifer was open to auditioning with Clooney. She tested by doing the sequence in which she and the bank robber on the lam are locked together in a car trunk. Jennifer describes, "George and I were in this office and we laid down together on a couch. We did the trunk scene and when we finished, I think I got it. I'll do that kind of stuff to get parts." In agreeing to make the picture, Lopez received a pay boost to $2 million.

Directed by Steven Soderbergh, *Out of Sight* was an engaging film. Critic Janet Maslin (*New York Times*) said that the picture, filled with colorful supporting characters, boasted costars who "take an intricate . . . crime tale and give it steam heat." Maslin praised Jennifer's performance, saying, "Ms. Lopez has her best movie role thus far, and she brings it both seductiveness and grit; if it was hard to imagine a hardworking, pistol-packing bombshell on the page, it couldn't be easier here."

For her impressive contributions to the picture, Jennifer received an Alma Award in the category of Outstanding Actress in a Feature Film in a Crossover Role. She was also nominated for two MTV Movie Awards: Best Screen Kiss and Best Female Performer.

Proving that Jennifer had risen noticeably up the ladder in the Hollywood film business, Jennifer was asked to be one of the actors (which included Woody Allen, Sharon Stone, Gene Hackman, Anne Bancroft, Danny Glover, and Sylvester Stallone) to provide voices for the full-length animated feature *Antz* (1998). Filled with impressive computer-generated animation, a witty script, and celebrity voices who fit their on-screen cartoon characters well, *Antz* took in more that $171 million in worldwide distribution.

Public Mistakes and a New Creative Direction

Whether making a splashy appearance with her husband Ojani Noa at the 1997 Academy Awards or being named one of *People* magazine's Fifty Most Beautiful People, Jennifer—with several major motion pictures now to her credit—was fast becoming a major show business celebrity. As such, she was interviewed by Stephen Rebello for the February 1998 issue of *Movieline* magazine.

Talking openly on many topics to the *Movieline* reporter, Jennifer not only discussed her blooming career, but she also made some unflattering remarks about some other performers. Among those Jennifer discussed were Gwyneth Paltrow, Winona Ryder, Cameron Diaz, Wesley Snipes, Madonna, and Jack Nicholson.

The *Movieline* article prompted many media sources to react quite negatively to Jennifer. This left her in an embarrassing position. In reaction, Jennifer apologized publicly for her comments and wrote personal notes of explanation to many of the targets of her verbal blunders. Meanwhile, several Hollywood figures—such as directors Gregory Nava and Stephen Soderbergh—came to Jennifer's defense with statements to the media. However, the damage had been done to Jennifer's once shiny image in Hollywood.

At this delicate time, Jennifer chose to lower her visibility until the situation calmed down. Besides, she wanted a change of pace after making one picture after another. It was at this point that she began to pursue a recording career. After a productive meeting with Sony MusicEntertainment's president Tommy Mottola, Lopez signed a contract with the major music company's Work Group label.

Jennifer's debut album, *On the 6* (a title derived from the number of the subway train Jennifer used to ride), was released in June 1999. In an interview with *Vibe* magazine (August 1999), Jennifer said of her debut album, "I can't try to be Whitney [Houston] or Faith [Evans]. I do something different. I have something else to offer to anybody who'll want to . . . get down."

Jennifer found success as a singer with the release of her debut album, On the 6, *which yielded several hit songs.* (Getty Images)

The album's 14 cuts included R&B tracks, Latin songs, and pop ballads. Jennifer co-wrote the songs "Should've Never" and "Too Late." She relied on such name music producers as Sean "Puffy" Combs, Emilio Estefan Jr., and Track Masters to give her album a smooth professional blend, aiming for a musical mix that equated to "Latin soul." For added interest, Jennifer performed a duet ("No Me Ames") with Latin singing star Marc Anthony.

Although the reviews in general for *On the 6* were only fair, Jennifer had a sizeable hit with the single "If You Had My Love," and the album rose to the top 10 of the *Billboard* music industry charts.

A Change of Heart

Within months of Jennifer's early 1997 marriage to Ojani Noa, the tabloids were reporting that the couple was experiencing domestic problems that included public disputes. Jennifer repeatedly denied these allegations, but soon there were rumors that Jennifer was interested romantically in Combs (also known as Puff Daddy or P. Diddy), a Harlem-born star of the hip-hop music scene and one of the producers of *On the 6*. This gossip of a new love interest was spurred by Jennifer's appearance in Combs's 1997 music video "Been Around the World," in which she performed a sultry dance with Sean.

Increasingly, Jennifer's career and interests kept her apart from Noa, who was working as the manager of the Conga Room, an L.A. club in which Jennifer was a financial backer. After Jennifer appeared at the March 1998 Oscars without her spouse, the press rushed to unravel the truth of her current status with Noa. Eventually it came out that Jennifer and Ojani had been separated since early 1998 and had actually divorced that March.

By fall 1999, with her first record album a commercial success and everyone aware of her divorce, Jennifer finally acknowledged that she and Sean were romantically involved.

On the night of December 26, 1999, Jennifer and Sean stopped at Club New York in Manhattan. During the evening one of Sean's associates was reputedly involved in a shooting on the premises. While police were reaching the crime scene, Sean and Jennifer made a speedy getaway in his vehicle. They screeched through 10 red lights before being corralled by law enforcers. While arresting the celebrity pair, as well as Combs's chauffeur and bodyguard, the police seized a stolen, loaded nine-millimeter gun found in the car. Jennifer was handcuffed and detained at the precinct for 14 hours before the charges were dropped and she was released.

Jennifer refused to blame Sean for this nightmarish situation. She loyally stood by him through the months after the arrest. He was exonerated in 2001 of any wrongdoing in this matter. However, by Valentine's Day that year, Lopez and Combs were no longer a couple.

Rebuilding Her Film Career Momentum

After a break of almost two years, Jennifer's next film was the August 2000 release *The Cell*. Jennifer received a $4 million salary for this science fiction/thriller entry.

Her character, a psychotherapist, has been experimenting with a new medical procedure. It allows her mind to actually enter that of her patients when they are in a catatonic state. Knowing of her breakthrough scientific work, an FBI agent implores her to take on a strange assignment. He requests her to enter the brain of a comatose dying serial killer and uncover where he has stashed his latest victim (who may still be alive). Creepy, dark, and visually engrossing—but at times absurdly farfetched—the film met with mixed reviews. Critics generally scoffed at the movie and its cast, but some fans were drawn to the entry's far-out premise—as well as the appeal of Lopez's journeying within a subject's mind.

In January 2001 Jennifer starred in the romantic comedy *The Wedding Planner.* For this role, Jennifer, who had proven her value as a costar of major movies, was paid $9 million. In the film she plays a hardworking wedding organizer who meets a handsome doctor (played by Matthew McConaughey) who discovers belatedly that the charming physician is the groom-to-be of one of her clients. As *The Wedding Planner* was opening in U.S. theaters to positive financial results, Jennifer's second record album, *J.Lo,* was released. With such cuts as "Love Don't Cost a Thing" the album soon shot up to number one on the music charts. This gave Jennifer the distinction of having a major hit movie and record album in distribution at the same time.

Adding to Jennifer's high visibility in 2001 was that she had a new escort in public. While making the music video to "Love Don't Cost a Thing" in October 2000, she had met dancer Cris Judd, who was a year older than she. The couple made a cozy appearance at the March 2001 Oscars. By late summer the duo announced their engagement. On September 29, 2001 at a lavish ceremony in California, the two were married before 170 family members and friends. Before long the couple were involved in building a huge

Jennifer performed hits from On the 6 *and her second album,* J.Lo, *at a televised concert in Puerto Rico in 2001.* (WireImage)

dream house high in the Hollywood Hills. That November her TV special, "Let's Get Loud—Jennifer Lopez," which had been taped in September at Roberto Clemente Stadium in Puerto Rico, aired on U.S. television.

7

LIVING THE GOOD LIFE

Thanks to Jennifer's visibility on the entertainment scene and her success in both film and music, she was now among the special group of Hollywood female actors who commanded top salaries. For $9 million, she starred in *Angel Eyes* (2001) as a tough Chicago police officer who is saved from a fatal ambush by a helpful stranger (played by Jim Caviezel).

Next Jennifer landed the lead role in *Enough* (2002). To play the woman fleeing with her young daughter from the clutches of her menacing husband, Jennifer was paid $10 million. Her character in the film refuses to be a victim, studying martial arts to defend herself. Jennifer worked with Wade Allen, an expert at Krav Maga (an Israeli fighting technique), to bring her up to speed—with grueling training—on this violent skill. Stephen Holden (*New York Times*) said of her performance, "Throughout, Ms. Lopez holds the screen in a star performance that has less to do with acting than with embodying a forceful, streetwise woman who stands up for herself."

Moving On

As a refreshing change of professional pace with *Enough,* Jennifer returned to romantic comedy in *Maid in Manhattan* (2002), for which Columbia Pictures raised her salary to $12 million. Capitalizing on her real-life background, Jennifer was well cast as a Puerto Rican–American from the Bronx. As Marisa Ventura, a single mother with a young son, she is a maid at a fancy midtown Manhattan hotel. Through a quirk of fate and a case of mistaken identity, a handsome politician (portrayed by Ralph Fiennes) thinks she is a chic hotel guest. Before long the seemingly ill-matched couple from two different lifestyles find they have much in common. *Maid in Manhattan* charmed audiences and grossed $93.8 million in North American distribution.

Meanwhile, proving that she was serious about continuing her recording career, Jennifer released her third album *J to Tha L-O!: The Remixes* (2002), which peaked at number one position on the *Billboard* album charts. By now Jennifer had expanded her business ventures to include a "sporty chic" dress line, a signature fragrance, greeting cards, and a restaurant in Pasadena, California

Jennifer signs an autograph for a young fan. (WireImage)

(which ex-husband Ojani Noa managed for a time), among other things.

While Jennifer's career was soaring in 2002, her personal life was taking a different turn. That June Jennifer announced that she and Cris Judd, her spouse of eight months, had recently separated and planned to terminate their union. The couple divorced in January 2003.

Ben Affleck

Continuing to top her previous screen salaries, Jennifer— as a replacement for Halle Berry—was given $12 million to star in *Gigli* (2003). This comedy teamed Lopez with Ben Affleck. An actor since childhood, Ben had shot to fame when he and Matt Damon shared an Academy Award for cowriting the screenplay to *Good Will Hunting* (1997), in which they costarred. A fun-loving soul, Ben was noted for being a thoughtful, sensitive personality on the sets of his pictures.

When the *Gigli* shoot was completed, Affleck placed an advertisement in the trade paper *Variety* in which he talked about Jennifer's "graciousness of spirit, beauty and courage, great empathy, astonishing talent, real poise and true grace." Despite this very public valentine to Jennifer, the couple insisted that their mutual admiration was professional and platonic.

By mid-2002, Jennifer had split from Cris Judd, and she and Ben were frequently tracked by the paparazzi while out on the town together. Meanwhile, to continue their working relationship, she agreed to costar with him in a relatively modestly budgeted comedy/drama, *Jersey Girl,* directed by independent filmmaker Kevin Smith.

As 2002 proceeded, Ben and Jen, as the tabloids called the lovebirds, monopolized the media's attention. News and photos of the couple—also referred to as Ben-Lo or Bennifer—documented their togetherness to a stunning degree. The tabloids insisted that Jennifer and Ben would soon marry.

Meanwhile Jennifer had acquired an eight-bedroom, 10,800-square-foot mansion on Biscayne Bay in Miami Beach for $9.5 million. In addition, following the release of *J to Tha L-O!: The Remixes* in early 2002, her fourth album, *This Is Me . . . Then*, came out in the fall. The popular CD reached the number two position on the *Billboard* music charts. The album spawned the hit single and music video "Jenny from the Block."

By November 2002 it was official that Lopez and Affleck were engaged. The media continuously speculated about when the wedding would occur. Then, in early 2004, the once-promising relationship between Ben and Jennifer fizzled out.

Picking Up the Pieces

In the midst of the overkill about Jennifer's romance with Ben Affleck, many wondered what had happened to *Gigli*, which had yet to be released. The picture had been previewed for test audiences and had not done well. The studio decided to trim scenes and reshoot the finale. Despite Columbia Pictures' efforts to fix the unreleased movie, *Gigli* had become an industry joke known to the general public. The 2003 box-office bomb earned a paltry $5.7 million before disappearing quickly from domestic distribution.

In the wake of the *Gigli* fiasco, Miramax Pictures temporarily shelved *Jersey Girl*. It was not until March 2004 that the picture was finally released. By then Jennifer's role had been reduced in screen time, and the plot had been restructured. In the film, Jennifer plays the wife of a hotshot New York City advertising executive (played by Affleck). Within the film's first 15 minutes she dies from complications during childbirth. Widower Affleck falls apart, unable to care for himself or his motherless baby girl. Retreating to his father's home in New Jersey, he eventually gains renewed spirit through meeting a new love. Some reviewers (including Roger Ebert of the *Chicago Sun-Times*) noted that Jennifer "is luminous in her few scenes."

With Lopez's two recent film missteps over with, the press turned their attention to the new man in Jennifer's life, Latin music superstar Marc Anthony, born Marco Antonio Muniz in New York City in 1969. As a teenager he broke into the music business as a background singer and then as a songwriter. Marc made his album debut with *When the Night Is Over* in 1991, which led to a series of increasingly popular discs (including 1995's *Todo a Su Tiempo*, 2001's *Libre*, and 2004's *Amar Sin Mentiras*). Over the years, Anthony had acted in feature films and had starred in a Broadway musical. With a former girlfriend, a member of the New York City police force, he had a daughter. From 2000 until June 2004, Marc was married to Dayanara Torres, the Puerto

Rican-born winner of the 1993 Miss Universe title. The couple has two children.

From the late 1990s onward, there had been recurrent rumors that Marc and Jennifer—who had worked together on occasional recordings and music videos—enjoyed a private relationship. The two denied such claims, but on June 5, 2004—four days after Marc divorced Dayanara in the Dominican Republic—he and Jennifer were married in secret at her Beverly Hills home. The 35 invited guests

Jennifer and her husband, singer Marc Anthony, perform at the 47th Annual Grammy Awards. (Landov)

included Jennifer's parents. The newlyweds were then ser-
enaded by Latin crooner Ricky Martin.

Later, when asked about her new domestic status,
Jennifer said, "I feel like this is my phase two, like it's a new
beginning. Like everything I did before really doesn't matter. . . . Maybe I was a little bit careless in the past. I'm not
a perfect person. I make mistakes. I just feel like I'm in a better place about who I am. I follow my heart. That's the one
thing I can say about myself. And I love that about myself."

Looking Ahead

In 2003 and 2004, Jennifer's film career was still moving
ahead at full force. Still being offered numerous roles, she
commanded a salary of $15 million per picture, a new high
for her. *An Unfinished Life,* made in 2003 and set for summer 2005 release by Miramax Pictures, pairs Jennifer with
Robert Redford. The film is a drama about a woman forced
by circumstances to move in with her estranged father-in-
law so that her daughter will have a stable environment. In
Shall We Dance? (2004), a romantic comedy from Miramax
Pictures based on a 1996 Japanese movie, Jennifer
costarred with Richard Gere in a tale of a bored accountant
who is inspired by a beautiful dance instructor to sign up
for lessons. In the New Line Cinema comedy *Monster-in-
Law* (2005), Jennifer is luckless in finding Mr. Right. When
she suddenly does discover him, the man's mother (played

by Jane Fonda) tries to destroy the budding relationship. Other big screen projects in the works include *Bordertown,* a crime drama set on the Texas/Mexico border, and *American Darlings,* which teams Jennifer with Nicole Kidman in a musical that is set in the swing scene in the days before World War II. Meanwhile, Lopez continued her music career with the release of her album *Rebirth* (2005) on the Epic label.

Jennifer Lopez can look back with satisfaction on her remarkable rise to fame. From the little girl watching *West Side Story* on TV in her Bronx home to the international superstar of A-list films and recordings, she has come a long way.

In building her film career, Jennifer says, "I always made the choice to do different things. I took the other role, the one that in the long run would mean more, even if it wasn't the one that might have put more money in the bank." She also believes, "You've got to do your share of commercial movies—romantic comedies, action movies—the $100 million movies, because if you don't, you're not going to have the power and Hollywood is not going to respect you. I would also do any small, independent movie that appeals to me dramatically, because it keeps everybody realizing that your acting chops are there. I think some actors are making a big mistake by doing one big commercial movie after another. It just looks like you're for sale. People want to know that you're selective."

Regarding her highly competitive nature, Jennifer admits, "I have this attitude—and it won't change no matter how big I get—that you have to fight for things you want!" As for the effect that fame has had on her, she says, "I don't think I've changed, but there is the aspect that people's perception of you changes when you become famous. It's weird how people treat you; it's a little strange. Somebody who obviously had faith once told me, 'When you become a star everybody around you is going to say you've changed, but it's not going to be you. What will change is everybody around you, the way they look at you.' I think there's an element of truth in that."

As to her career future, Jennifer, who has her own film production company (Nuyorican Productions) acknowledges, "I still wake up thinking about everything that I want to achieve . . . feeling that I can't stop . . . that I have to win an Oscar . . . make better movies . . . sing in big arenas. . . . Every day I wake up with that anxiety."

While Jennifer Lopez remains continually ambitious about expanding her professional success, there is one other area, in particular, where she has already accomplished much. By persevering in her show business and music careers and becoming so successful, her example has created a great deal of positive visibility for Latin performers. By avoiding stereotypical acting roles that for so long were thrust on ethnic minorities, Jennifer has demonstrated that talented, determined performers can rise above racial barriers and make a distinct impression on the world on their own terms.

TIME LINE

1970 Jennifer Lopez born in the Bronx, New York, on July 24; the second of three children

1976 Begins taking dance classes

1986 Makes feature film debut in *My Little Girl* (Hemdale), shot in Philadelphia

1987 Graduates from Preston High School in the Bronx; attends classes at Baruch College in Manhattan but drops out after one semester

1988 Begins dancing professionally in music videos and at New York City clubs; later tours Europe with the revue *Golden Musicals of Broadway,* performs in Japan in the show *Synchronicity*

1991 Selected to be a Fly Girl on Fox TV's variety show *In Living Color*; relocates to Los Angeles

1993   Leaves *In Living Color* to pursue acting roles; TV
movie: *Nurses on the Line: The Crash of Flight 7*
(CBS); TV series: *Second Chances* (CBS)

1994   TV series: *Hotel Malibu* (CBS) and *South Central*
(Fox)

1995   Hired by director Gregory Nava for the feature film
My Family/Mi Familia (New Line Cinema); ends
long-term relationship with boyfriend David Cruz;
other film: *Money Train* (Columbia)

1996   Films: *Jack* (Buena Vista); *Blood and Wine* (Fox
Searchlight)

1997   With her $1 million salary for starring in *Selena*
(Warner Bros.), becomes the highest-paid Latina
performer in Hollywood history and earns a Golden
Globe Award nomination for her screen performance; other films: *Anaconda* (Columbia), and *U-Turn*
(TriStar); in February weds waiter/model Ojani Noa
in Florida

1998   Earns $2 million to costar with George Clooney in
Out of Sight (Universal); signs recording contract
with Sony Records; other film: *Antz* (DreamWorks);
divorces Ojani Noa; begins dating rap entrepre-
neur/singer Sean "Puffy" Combs

1999 Debut album, *On the 6,* is released by Sony and becomes a hit; Lopez makes headlines in December when detained (and eventually released) by New York City police regarding a shooting at Manhattan club she visited with Sean "Puffy" Combs

2000 Named Female Entertainer of the Year by the ALMA Awards; film: *The Cell* (New Line Cinema)

2001 Now earning $9 million per movie; films: *The Wedding Planner* (Columbia) and *Angel Eyes* (Warner Bros.); albums: *J.Lo* (Sony); TV concert: "Let's Get Loud—Jennifer Lopez" (NBC); ends relationship with Sean "Puffy" Combs; in September marries dancer/choreographer Cris Judd in Los Angeles

2002 Salary escalates to $12 million per feature film; expands business enterprises to include clothing line fragrance, and a Pasadena, California–based restaurant (Madre); albums: *J to Tha L-O!: The Remixes* (Epic) and *This Is Me . . . Then* (Epic); films: *Enough* (Columbia) and *Maid in Manhattan* (Columbia); meets actor Ben Affleck; separates from Cris Judd

2003 DVDs: *Reel Me* (Sony); film: *Gigli* (Columbia); divorces Cris Judd; personal relationship with Ben Affleck generates tremendous media blitz

2004   Films: *Jersey Girl* (Miramax) and *Shall We Dance?* (Miramax); ends romance with Ben Affleck; in June marries superstar singer Marc Anthony in Los Angeles

2005   Now earning $15 million per movie; album: *Rebirth* (Epic); films: *Monster-In-Law* (New Line Cinema), *An Unfinished Life* (Miramax), *Bordertown* (in production), *American Darlings* (in production)

HOW TO BECOME AN ACTOR

THE JOB

The imitation or basic development of a character for presentation to an audience may seem like a glamorous and fairly easy job. In reality, it is demanding, tiring work that requires a special talent.

An actor must first find an available part in some upcoming production. This may be in a comedy, drama, musical, or opera. Then, having read and studied the part, the actor must audition before the director and other people who have control of the production. This requirement is often waived for established artists. In film and television, actors must also complete screen tests, which are scenes recorded on film, at times performed with other actors, which are later viewed by the director and producer of the film.

If selected for the part, the actor must spend hundreds of hours in rehearsal and must memorize many lines and cues. This is especially true in live theater; in film and television actors may spend less time in rehearsal and sometimes improvise their lines before the camera, often performing several attempts, or "takes," before the director is satisfied. Television actors often take advantage of TelePrompTers, which scroll lines on a screen in front of performing actors. Radio actors generally read from a script, and therefore their rehearsal times are usually shorter.

In addition to such mechanical duties, the actor must determine the essence of the character he or she is auditioning for, and the relation of that character to the overall scheme of the production. Radio actors must be especially skilled in expressing character and emotion through voice alone. In many film and theater roles, actors must also sing and dance and spend additional time rehearsing songs and perfecting choreography. Certain roles require actors to perform various stunts, some of which can be quite dangerous. Specially trained performers usually complete these stunts. Others work as stand-ins or body doubles. These actors are chosen for specific features and appear on film in place of the lead actor; this is often the case in films requiring nude or seminude scenes. Many television programs, such as game shows, also feature models, who generally assist the host of the program.

Actors in the theater may perform the same part many times a week for weeks, months, and sometimes years. This allows them to develop the role, but it can also become tedious. Actors in films may spend several weeks involved in a production, which often takes place on location (that is, in different parts of the world). Television actors involved in a series, such as a soap opera or a situation comedy, also may play the same role for years, generally in 13-week cycles. For these actors, however, their lines change from week to week and even from day to day, and much time is spent rehearsing their new lines.

While studying and perfecting their craft, many actors work as extras, the nonspeaking characters who appear in the background on screen or stage. Many actors also continue training throughout their careers. A great deal of an actor's time is spent attending auditions.

REQUIREMENTS
High School
There are no minimum educational requirements to become an actor. However, at least a high school diploma is recommended. In high school English classes you will learn about the history of drama and the development of

strong characters. Take music classes to help you develop your voice and ability to read music, which are valuable skills for any actor, even those who do not perform many musical roles.

Postsecondary Training

A college degree is becoming more important for those who hope to have an acting career. An actor who has completed a liberal arts program is thought to be more capable of understanding the wide variety of roles that are available. Therefore, it is strongly recommended that aspiring actors complete at least a bachelor's degree program in theater or the dramatic arts. In addition, graduate degrees in the fine arts or in drama are nearly always required should the individual decide to teach dramatic arts.

College can also provide acting experience for the hopeful actor. More than 500 colleges and universities throughout the country offer dramatic arts programs and present theatrical performances. Actors and directors recommend that those interested in acting gain as much experience as possible through acting in high school and college plays or in those offered by community groups. Training beyond college is recommended, especially for actors interested in entering the theater. Joining acting workshops, such as the Actors Studio, can often be highly competitive.

Other Requirements

Prospective actors will be required not only to have a great talent for acting but also a great determination to succeed in the theater and motion pictures. They must be able to memorize hundreds of lines and should have a good speaking voice. The ability to sing and dance is important for increasing the opportunities for the young actor. Almost all actors are required to audition for a part before they receive the role. In film and television, actors will generally complete screen tests to see how they appear on film. In all fields of acting, a love of performing is a must. It might take many years for an actor to achieve any success, if they achieve it at all.

Performers on Broadway stages must be members of the Actors' Equity Association before being cast. While union membership may not always be required, many actors find it advantageous to belong to a union that covers their particular field of performing arts. These organizations include the Actors' Equity Association (stage), Screen Actors Guild or Screen Extras Guild (motion pictures and television films), or American Federation of Television and Radio Artists (TV, recording, and radio). In addition, some actors may benefit from membership in the American Guild of Variety Artists (nightclubs and so on), American Guild of Musical Artists (opera and ballet), or organizations such as the Hebrew Actors

Union or Italian Actors Union for productions in those languages.

EXPLORING

The best way to explore this career is to participate in school or local theater productions. Even working on the props or lighting crew will provide insight into the field.

Also, attend as many dramatic productions as possible, and try to talk with people who either are currently in the theater or have been at one time. They can offer advice to individuals interested in a career in the theater.

There are many books about acting that concern not only how to perform, but also the nature of the work, its offerings, advantages, and disadvantages.

EMPLOYERS

Motion pictures, television, and the stage are the largest fields of employment for actors, with television commercials representing as much as 60 percent of all acting jobs. Most of the opportunities for employment in these fields are either in Los Angeles or in New York. On the stage, even the road shows often have their beginning in New York, with the selection of actors conducted there, along with rehearsals. However, nearly every city and most communities present local and regional theater productions.

As cable television networks continue to produce more and more of their own programs and films, they will become a major provider of employment for actors. Home video will also continue to create new acting jobs, as will the music video business.

The lowest numbers of actors are employed for stage work. In addition to Broadway shows and regional theater, there are employment opportunities for stage actors in summer stock, at resorts, and on cruise ships.

STARTING OUT

Probably the best way to enter acting is to start with high school, local, or college productions and gain as much experience as possible on that level. Very rarely is an inexperienced actor given an opportunity to perform onstage or in a film in New York or Hollywood. The field is extremely difficult to enter; the more experience and ability beginners have, however, the greater the possibilities for entrance.

Those venturing to New York or Hollywood are encouraged first to have enough money to support themselves during the long waiting and searching period typically required before a job is found. Most will list themselves with a casting agency that will help them find a part as an extra or a bit player, either in theater or film. These agencies keep names on file along with photographs and a description of the individual's features and experience, and if a part comes along that may be suitable, they contact that person. Very often, however, names are added to their lists only when the number of people in a particular physical category is low. For instance, the agency may not have enough athletic young women on its roster, and if the applicant happens to fit this description, her name is added.

ADVANCEMENT

New actors will typically start with bit parts and will have only a few lines to speak, if any. The normal progression would then be landing larger supporting roles and then, in the case of theater, possibly a role as an understudy for one of the main actors. The understudy usually has an opportunity to fill in if the main actor is unable to give a performance. Many film and television actors get their start in commercials or by appearing in government and commercially sponsored public service announcements, films, and programs. Other actors join the afternoon soap operas and continue on to evening programs. Many actors also have started in on-camera roles such as presenting the weather segment of a local news program. Once an actor has gained experience, he or she may go on to play stronger supporting roles or even leading roles in stage, television, or film productions. From there, an actor may go on to stardom. Only a very small number of actors ever reach that pinnacle, however.

Some actors eventually go into other, related occupations and become drama coaches, drama teachers, producers, stage directors, motion picture directors, television directors, radio directors, stage managers, casting directors, or artist and repertoire managers. Others may combine one or more of these functions while continuing their careers.

EARNINGS

The wage scale for actors is largely controlled through bargaining agreements reached by various unions in negotiations with producers. These agreements typically control the minimum salaries, hours of work permitted per week, and other conditions of employment. In addition, each artist enters into a separate contract that may provide for higher salaries.

In 2003, the minimum daily salary of any member of the Screen Actors Guild (SAG) in a speaking role was $678 or $2,352 for a five-day workweek. Motion picture actors may also receive additional payments known as residuals as part of their guaranteed salary. Many motion picture actors receive residuals whenever films, TV shows, and TV commercials in which they appear are rerun, sold for TV exhibition, or put on videocassette. Residuals often exceed the actor's original salary and account for about one-third of all actors' income.

A wide range of earnings can be seen when reviewing the Actors' Equity Association's *Annual Report 2003,* which includes a breakdown of average weekly salaries by contract type and location. According to the report, for example, actors in off-Broadway productions earned an average weekly salary of $700 during the 2002–03 season. Other average weekly earnings for the same period include: San Francisco Bay area theater, $318; New England area theater, $294; DisneyWorld in Orlando, Florida, $683; and Chicago area theater, $487. The report concludes that the median weekly salary for all contract areas is $487. Most actors do not work 52 weeks per year; in fact, the report notes that the 39,981 Equity members in good standing only worked an average 16.4 weeks during the 2002–03 season, with median earnings of $6,418.

According to the U.S. Department of Labor, the median yearly earning of all actors was $26,460 in 2003. The department also reported the lowest paid 10 percent earned less than $13,380 annually, while the highest paid 10 percent made more than $120,210.

The annual earnings of persons in television and movies are affected by frequent periods of unemployment. According to SAG, most of its members earn less than $7,500 a year from acting jobs. Unions offer health, welfare, and pension funds for members working more than a set number of weeks a year. Some actors are eligible for paid vacation and sick time, depending on the work contract.

In all fields, well-known actors have salary rates above the minimums, and the salaries of the few top stars are many times higher. Actors in television series may earn tens of thousands of dollars per week, while a few may earn as much as $1 million or more per week. Salaries for these actors vary considerably and are negotiated individually. In film, top stars may earn as much as $20 million per film, and, if they also receive a percentage of the gross earned by the film, these stars can earn far, far more.

Until recent years, female film stars tended to earn lower salaries than their male counterparts; stars such as Julia Roberts, Hillary Swank, Halle Berry, and others have started to reverse that trend. The average annual earnings for all motion picture actors, however, are usually low for all but the best-known performers because of the periods of unemployment.

WORK ENVIRONMENT

Actors work under varying conditions. Those employed in motion pictures may work in air-conditioned studios one week and be on location in a hot desert the next.

Those in stage productions perform under all types of conditions. The number of hours employed per day or week varies, as does the number of weeks employed per year. Stage actors typically perform eight shows per week; any additional performances are compensated with overtime pay. The basic workweek after the show opens is about 36 hours, unless major changes in the play are needed. The number of hours worked per week is considerably more before the opening-night performance because of rehearsals. Evening work is a natural part of a stage actor's life. Rehearsals often are held at night and over holidays and weekends. If the play goes on the road, much traveling will be involved.

A number of actors cannot receive unemployment compensation when they are waiting for their next part, primarily because they have not worked enough hours to meet the minimum eligibility requirements for compensation. Sick leaves and paid vacations are not usually available to the actor. However, union actors who earn the minimum qualifications now receive full medical and health insurance under all the actors' unions. Those who earn health-plan benefits for 10 years become eligible for a pension upon retirement. The acting field is very uncertain. Aspirants never know whether they will be able to get into the profession, and, once in, an actor cannot be certain that his or her show will be well received—if it's not, it also cannot be predicted whether the actors' career will survive a bad show.

OUTLOOK

Employment in acting is expected to grow about as fast as average through 2012, according to the U.S. Department of Labor. There are a number of reasons for this. The growth of satellite and cable television in the past decade has created a demand for more actors, especially as the cable networks produce more and more of their own programs and films. The rise of home video has also created new acting jobs, as more and more films are made strictly for the home video market. Many resorts built in the 1980s and 1990s present their own theatrical productions, providing more job opportunities for actors. Jobs in theater, however, face pressure as the cost of mounting a production rises and as many nonprofit and smaller theaters lose their funding.

Despite the growth in opportunities, there are many more actors than there are roles, and this is likely to remain true for years to come. This is true in all areas of the arts, including radio, television, motion pictures, and theater, and even those who are employed are typically employed during only a small portion of the year. Many actors must supplement their income by working in other capacities, for instance as secretaries, waiters, or taxi drivers. Almost all performers are members of more than one union in order to take advantage of various opportunities as they become available.

It should be recognized that of the 139,000 or so actors in the United States today, only a small percentage are working as actors at any one time. Of these, few are able to support themselves on their earnings from acting, and fewer still will ever achieve stardom. Most actors work for many years before becoming known, and most of these do not rise above supporting roles. The vast majority of actors, meanwhile, are still looking for the right break. There are many more applicants in all areas than there are positions. As with most careers in the arts, people enter this career out of a love and desire to practice the craft.

TO LEARN MORE ABOUT ACTORS

BOOKS

Bruder, Melissa. *A Practical Handbook for the Actor.* New York: Vintage, 1986.

Lee, Robert L. *Everything about Theater!: The Guidebook of Theater Fundamentals.* Colorado Springs, Colo.: Meriwether, 1996.

Quinlan, Kathryn A. *Actor.* Mankato, Minn.: Capstone Press, 1998.

Stevens, Chambers. *Magnificent Monologues for Kids.* South Pasadena, Calif.: Sandcastle, 1999.

ORGANIZATIONS

The Actors' Equity Association is a professional union for actors in theater and "live" industrial productions, as well as stage managers, some directors, and choreographers.

Actors' Equity Association
165 West 46th Street
New York, NY 10036
Tel: 212-869-8530
E-mail: info@actorsequity.org
http://www.actorsequity.org

This union represents television and radio performers, including actors, announcers, dancers, disc jockeys, newspersons, singers, specialty acts, sportscasters, and stuntpersons.

American Federation of Television and Radio Artists
260 Madison Avenue
New York, NY 10016-2402
Tel: 212-532-0800
E-mail: aftra@aftra.com
http://www.aftra.com

A directory of theatrical programs may be purchased from NAST. For answers to a number of frequently asked questions concerning education, visit the NAST website.

National Association of Schools of Theater (NAST)
11250 Roger Bacon Drive, Suite 21
Reston, VA 20190
Tel: 703-437-0700
E-mail: info@arts-accredit.org
http://www.arts-accredit.org/nast

The Screen Actors Guild (SAG) provides general information on actors, directors, and producers. Visit the SAG website for more information.

Screen Actors Guild (SAG)
5757 Wilshire Boulevard
Los Angeles, CA 90036-3600
Tel: 323-954-1600
http://www.sag.com

For information about opportunities in not-for-profit theaters, contact the Theater Communications Group.

Theatre Communications Group
355 Lexington Avenue
New York, NY 10017
Tel: 212-697-5230
E-mail: tcg@tcg.org
http://www.tcg.org

This site has information for beginners on acting and the acting business.

Acting Workshop On-Line

http://www.redbirdstudio.com/AWOL/acting2.html

HOW TO BECOME A SINGER

THE JOB

Singers are employed to perform music with their voices by using their knowledge of vocal sound and delivery, harmony, melody, and rhythm. They put their individual vocal styles into the songs they sing, and they interpret music accordingly. The inherent sounds of the voices in a performance play a significant part in how a song will affect an audience; this essential aspect of a singer's voice is known as its tone.

Classical singers are usually categorized according to the range and quality of their voices, beginning with the highest singing voice, the soprano, and ending with the lowest, the bass; voices in between include mezzo soprano, contralto, tenor, and baritone. Singers perform either alone (in which case they are referred to as *soloists*) or as members of an ensemble, or group. They sing by either following a score, which is the printed musical text, or by memorizing the material. Also, they may sing either with or without instrumental accompaniment; singing without accompaniment is called *a cappella*. In opera— which are plays set to music—singers perform the various roles, much as actors do, interpreting the drama with their voice to the accompaniment of a symphony orchestra.

Classical singers may perform a variety of musical styles or specialize in a specific period; they may give recitals or perform as members of an ensemble. Classical singers generally undergo years of voice training and instruction in musical theory. They develop their vocal technique and learn how to project without harming their voices. Classical singers rarely use a microphone when they sing; nonetheless, their voices must be heard above the music provide by the orchestra. Because classical singers often perform music from many different languages, they learn how to pronounce these languages, and often how to speak them as well. Those who are involved in operatic performance work for opera companies in major cities throughout the country and often travel extensively. Some classical singers also perform in other musical areas.

Professional singers tend to perform in a chosen style of music, such as jazz, rock, or blues, among many others. Many singers pursue careers that will lead them to perform for coveted recording contracts, on concert tours, and for television and motion pictures. Others perform in rock, pop, country, gospel, or folk groups, singing in concert halls, nightclubs, and churches and at social gatherings and for small studio recordings. Whereas *virtuosos*, classical artists who are expertly skilled in their singing style, tend to perform traditional pieces that have been handed down through hundreds of years, singers in other areas often perform popular, contemporary pieces, and often songs that they themselves have composed.

Another style of music in which formal training is often helpful is jazz. *Jazz singers* learn phrasing, breathing, and vocal techniques; often the goal of a jazz singer is to make his or her voice as much a part of the instrumentation as the piano, saxophone, trumpet, or trombone. Many jazz singers perform *scat* singing, in which the voice is used in an improvisational way much like any other instrument.

Folk singers perform songs that may be many years old, or they may write their own songs. Folk singers generally perform songs that express a certain cultural tradition. While some folk singers specialize in their own or another culture, others may sing songs from a great variety of cultural and musical traditions. In the United States, folk singing is particularly linked to the acoustic guitar, and many singers accompany themselves with guitar while singing.

A cappella singing, which is singing without musical accompaniment, takes many forms. A cappella music may be a part of classical music; it may also be a part of folk music, as in the singing of barbershop quartets. Another form, called doo-wop, is closely linked to rock and rhythm-and-blues music.

Gospel music, which evolved in the United States, is a form of sacred music; *gospel singers* generally sing as part of a choir, accompanied by an organ, or other musical instruments, but may also perform a cappella. Many popular singers began their careers as singers in church and gospel choirs before entering jazz, pop, blues, or rock.

Pop/rock singers generally require no formal training whatsoever. Rock music is a very broad term encompassing many different styles of music, such as heavy metal, punk, rap, rhythm and blues, rockabilly, techno, and many others. Many popular rock singers cannot sing well in the traditional, trained sense. But rock singers learn to express themselves and their music, developing their own phrasing and vocal techniques. Rock singers usually sing as part of a band, or with a backing band to accompany them. Rock singers usually sing with microphones so that they can be heard above the amplified instruments around them.

All singers practice and rehearse their songs and music. Some singers read from music scores while performing; others perform from memory. Yet all must gain an intimate knowledge of their music, so that they can best convey its meanings and feelings to their audience. Singers must also exercise their voices even when not performing. Some singers perform as featured soloists and artists. Others perform as part of a choir, or as backup singers adding harmony to the lead singer's voice.

REQUIREMENTS

High School

Many singers require no formal training in order to sing. However, those interested in becoming classical or jazz singers should begin learning and honing their talent when they are quite young. Vocal talent can be recognized in grade school students and even in younger children. In general, however, these early years are a time of vast development and growth in singing ability. Evident changes occur in the voices of boys' and girls' when they are around 12 to 14 years old, during which time their vocal cords go through a process of lengthening and thickening. Although boys' voices tend to change much more so than girls' voices, both genders should be provided with challenges that will help them achieve their talent goals. Young students should learn about breath control and why it is necessary; they should learn to follow a conductor, and understand the relationship between the conductor's hand and baton motions and the dynamics of the music; and they should learn about musical concepts such as tone, melody, harmony, and rhythm.

During the last two years of high school, aspiring singers should have a good idea of what classification they are in, according to the range and quality of their voices: soprano, alto, contralto, tenor, baritone, or bass. These categories indicate the resonance of the voice; soprano being the highest and lightest, bass being the lowest and heaviest. Students should take part in voice classes, choirs, and ensembles. In addition, students should continue their studies in English, writing, social studies, foreign language, and other electives in music, theory, and performance.

There tend to be no formal educational requirements for those who wish to be singers. However, formal education is valuable, especially in younger years. Some students know early in their lives that they want to be singers and are ambitious enough to continue to practice and learn. These students are often advised to attend high schools that are specifically geared toward combined academic and intensive arts education in music, dance, and theater. Such schools can provide valuable preparation and guidance for those who plan to pursue professional careers in the arts. Admission is usually based on results from students' auditions as well as academic testing.

Postsecondary Training

Many find it worthwhile and fascinating to continue their study of music and voice in a liberal arts program at a college or university. Similarly, others attend schools of higher education that are focused specifically on music, such as the Juilliard School (http://www.juilliard.edu) in New York. Such an intense program would include a multidisciplinary curriculum of composition and performance, as well as study and appreciation of the history, development, variety, and potential advances of music. In this type of program, a student would earn a Bachelor of Arts degree. To earn a Bachelor of Science degree in music, one would study musicology, which concerns the history, literature, and cultural background of music; the music industry, which will prepare one for not only singing but also marketing music and other business aspects; and professional performance. Specific music classes in a typical four-year liberal arts program would include such courses as introduction to music; music styles and structures; harmony; theory of music; elementary and advanced auditory training; music history; and individual instruction.

In addition to learning at schools, many singers are taught by *private singing teachers* and *voice coaches,* who help to develop and refine students' voices. Many aspiring singers take courses at continuing adult education centers, where they can take advantage of courses in beginning and advanced singing, basic vocal techniques, voice coaching, and vocal performance workshops. When one is involved in voice training, he or she must learn about good articulation and breath control, which are very important qualities for all singers. Performers must take care of their voices and keep their lungs in good condition. Voice training, whether as part of a college curriculum or in private study, is useful to many singers, not only for classical and opera singers, but also for jazz singers and for those interested in careers in musical theater. Many professional singers who have already "made it" continue to take voice lessons throughout their careers.

Other Requirements

As with other areas of music, learning to sing and becoming a singer is often a matter of desire, practice, and an inborn love and talent for the craft. Learning to play a musical instrument is often extremely helpful in learning to sing and to read and write music. Sometimes it is not even necessary to have a "good" singing voice. Many singers in rock music have less-than-perfect voices, and rap artists do not really sing at all. Nonetheless, these singers learn to use their voices to express their songs, music, and ideas in artistic and innovative ways.

EXPLORING

Anyone who is interested in pursuing a career as a singer should obviously have a love for music. Listen to recordings as often as possible, and get an understanding of the types of music that you enjoy. Singing, alone or with family and friends, is one of the most natural ways to explore music and develop a sense of your own vocal style. Join music clubs at school as well as the school band if it does vocal performances. In addition, take part in school drama productions that involve musical numbers.

Older students interested in classical music careers could contact trade associations such as the American Guild of Musical Artists. They should also read trade journals such as *Hot Line News* (published by Musicians National Hot Line Association), which covers news about singers and other types of musicians and their employment needs and opportunities. For information and news about very popular singers, read *Billboard* magazine (http://www.billboard.com), which can be purchased at many local bookshops and newsstands. Those who already know what type of music they wish to sing should audition for roles in community musical productions or contact trade groups that offer competitions. For example, the Central Opera Service (Metropolitan Opera, Lincoln Center, New York, NY 10023) can provide information on competitions, apprentice programs, and performances for young singers interested in opera.

There are many summer programs offered throughout the United States for high school students interested in singing and other performing arts. (See the end of this article for contact information on these programs.) For example, Stanford University offers its Stanford Jazz Workshop each summer for students who are 12 years old and up. It offers activities in instrumental and vocal music, as well as recreation in swimming, tennis, and volleyball. For college students who are 18 and older, the jazz workshop has a number of positions available.

Another educational facility that provides a summer program is Boston University's Tanglewood Institute, which is geared especially toward very talented and ambitious students between the ages of 15 and 18. It offers sessions in chorus, musical production, chamber music, classical music, ensemble, and vocal practice. Arts and culture field trips are also planned. College students who are 20 and older can apply for available jobs at the summer Tanglewood programs.

Students interested in other areas of singing can begin practicing and performing while still in high school, or even sooner. Many gospel singers, for example, start singing with their local church group at an early age. Many high school students form their own bands, playing rock, country, or jazz, and can gain experience performing before an audience; some of these young musicians even get paid to perform at school parties and other social functions.

EMPLOYERS

There are many different environments in which singers can be employed, including local lounges, bars, cafes, cruise ships, resorts, hotels, and casinos. They can also participate in large concert tours and in radio, television, theater, and opera productions.

Many singers hire agents, who usually receive a percentage of the singer's earnings for finding them appropriate performance contracts. Others are employed primarily as *studio singers,* which means that they do not perform for live audiences but rather record their singing in studios for albums, radio broadcasts, television shows, motion pictures, and commercials.

An important tactic for finding employment as a singer is to invest in a professional-quality tape recording of your singing that you can send to prospective employers.

STARTING OUT

There is no single correct way of entering the singing profession. It is recommended that aspiring singers explore the avenues that interest them, continuing to apply and audition for whatever medium suits them. Singing is an extremely creative profession, and singers must learn to be creative and resourceful in the business matters of finding gigs.

High school students should seek out any opportunities to perform, including choirs, school musical productions, and church and other religious functions. Singing teachers can arrange recitals and introduce students to their network of musician contacts.

ADVANCEMENT

In the singing profession and the music industry in general, the nature of the business is such that singers can consider themselves to have made it when they get steady, full-time work. A measure of advancement is how well known and respected singers become in their field, which in turn influences their earnings. In most areas, particularly classical music, only the most talented and persistent singers make it to the top of their profession. In other areas, success may be largely a matter of luck and perseverance. A singer on Broadway, for example, may begin as a member of the chorus and eventually become a featured singer. On the other hand, those who have a certain passion for their work and accept their career position tend to enjoy working in local performance centers, nightclubs, and other musical environments.

Also, many experienced singers who have had formal training will become voice teachers. Reputable schools such as Juilliard consider it a plus when a student can say that he or she has studied with a master.

EARNINGS

As with many occupations in the performing arts, earnings for singers are highly dependent on one's professional reputation and thus cover a wide range. To some degree, pay is also related to educational background (as it relates to how well one has been trained) and geographic location of performances. In certain situations, such as singing for audio recordings, pay is dependent on the number of minutes of finished music (for instance, an hour's pay will be given for each three and a half minutes of recorded song).

Singing is often considered a glamorous occupation. However, because it attracts so many professionals, competition for positions is very high. Only a small proportion of those who aspire to be singers achieve glamorous jobs and extremely lucrative contracts. Famous opera singers, for example earn $8,000 and more for each performance.

Singers in an opera chorus earn between $600 and $800 per week. Classical soloists can receive between $2,000 and $3,000 per performance, while choristers may receive around $70 per performance. For rock singers, earnings can be far higher. Within the overall group of professional singers, studio and opera singers tend to earn salaries that are well respected in the industry; their opportunities for steady, long-term contracts tend to be better than for singers in other areas.

Average salaries for musicians, singers, and related workers were $37,380 in 2003, according to the U.S. Department of Labor. The lowest paid 10 percent earned less than $13,110 per year, while the highest paid 10 percent earned more than $110,930 annually.

Because singers rarely work for a single employer, they generally receive no fringe benefits and must provide their own health insurance and retirement planning.

WORK ENVIRONMENT

The environments in which singers work tend to vary greatly, depending on such factors as type of music involved and location of performance area. Professional singers often work in the evenings and during weekends, and many are frequently required to travel. Many singers who are involved in popular productions such as in opera, rock, and country music work in large cities such as New

York, Las Vegas, Chicago, Los Angeles, and Nashville. Stamina and endurance are needed to keep up with the hours of rehearsals and performances, which can be long; work schedules are very often erratic, varying from job to job.

Many singers are members of trade unions, which represent them in matters such as wage scales and fair working conditions. Vocal performers who sing for studio recordings are represented by the American Federation of Television and Radio Artists; solo opera singers, solo concert singers, and choral singers are members of the American Guild of Musical Artists.

OUTLOOK

Any employment forecast for singers will most probably emphasize one factor that plays an important role in the availability of jobs: competition. Because so many people pursue musical careers and because there tend to be no formal requirements for employment in this industry (the main qualification is talent), competition is most often very strong.

According to the U.S. Department of Labor, employment for singers, as for musicians in general, is expected to grow about as fast as the average for all other occupations through 2012. The entertainment industry is expected to grow during the next decade, which will create jobs for singers and other performers. Because of the nature of this work, positions tend to be temporary and part time; in fact, of all members of the American Federation of Musicians, fewer than 2 percent work full time in their singing careers. Thus it is often advised that those who are intent on pursuing a singing career keep in mind the varied fields other than performance in which their interest in music can be beneficial, such as composition, education, broadcasting, therapy, and community arts management.

Those intent on pursuing singing careers in rock, jazz, and other popular forms should be aware of the keen competition they will face. There are thousands of singers all hoping to make it; only a very few actually succeed. However, there are many opportunities to perform in local cities and communities, and those with a genuine love of singing and performing should also possess a strong sense of commitment and dedication to their art.

TO LEARN MORE ABOUT SINGERS

BOOKS

Baxter, Marc. *The Rock-n-Roll Singer's Survival Guide.* Milwaukee, Wis.: Hal Leonard, 1990.

Emmons, Shirlee, and Alma Thomas. *Power Performance for Singers: Transcending the Barriers.* New York: Oxford University Press, 1998.

Hewitt, Graham. *How to Sing.* New York: Taplinger Publishing, 1979.

Murray, Dena. *Vocal Techniques: A Guide to Finding Your Real Voice.* Hollywood: Musicians Institute Press, 2002.

Peckham, Anne. *The Contemporary Singer: Elements of Vocal Technique.* Boston: Berklee Press, 2000.

ORGANIZATIONS AND WEBSITES

For information on membership in a local union nearest you, developments in the music field, a searchable database of U.S. and foreign music schools, and articles on careers in music, visit the following website.

American Federation of Musicians of the United States and Canada
1501 Broadway, Suite 600
New York, NY 10036
Tel: 212-869-1330
http://www.afm.org

For information on union membership, contact the American Federation of Television and Radio Artists.

American Federation of Television and Radio Artists
260 Madison Avenue
New York, NY 10016-2401
Tel: 212-532-0800
E-mail: info@aftra.com
http://www.aftra.com

The AGMA is a union for professional musicians. Their website has information on upcoming auditions, news announcements for the field, and membership information.

American Guild of Musical Artists (AGMA)
1430 Broadway, 14th Floor
New York, NY 10018
Tel: 212-265-3687
E-mail: AGMA@MusicalArtists.org
http://www.musicalartists.org

For a list of colleges and universities that offer music-related programs, contact the National Association of Schools of Music.

National Association of Schools of Music
11250 Roger Bacon Drive, Suite 21
Reston, VA 20190
Tel: 703-437-0700
E-mail: info@arts-accredit.org
http://nasm.arts-accredit.org

TO LEARN MORE ABOUT JENNIFER LOPEZ

BOOKS

Baker, Trevor. *Jennifer Lopez*. London: Carlton, 2001*

Duncan, Patricia J. *Jennifer Lopez: An Unauthorized Biography*. New York: St. Martin's, 1999.

Furman, Leah and Elina Furman. *Jennifer Lopez*. Philadelphia: Chelsea House, 2001.*

Gale Group. *Contemporary Theatre, Film and Television*. Vol. 31. Farmington Hills, Mich.: Gale, 2000.

Gallick, Sarah. *J.Lo: The Secrets Behind Jennifer Lopez's Climb to the Top*. Boca Raton, Fla.: AMI Books, Inc., 2003.

Henderson, Ashyia N. (project ed.). *Contemporary Hispanic Biography.* Vol. 1. Farmington Hills, Mich.: Gale, 2002.

Hill, Anne E. *Jennifer Lopez.* Philadelphia: Chelsea House, 2000.*

Hurst, Heidi. *Jennifer Lopez.* San Diego: Lucent, 2003.*

Johns, Michael-Anne. *Jennifer Lopez.* Kansas City, Mo.: Andrews McMeel, 2000.

Menard, Valerie. *Jennifer Lopez.* Bear, Del.: Mitchell Lane, 2003.*

Parish, James Robert. *Hollywood Bad Boys.* Chicago: Contemporary, 2002.

_____. *Hollywood Divas.* Chicago: Contemporary, 2003.

Parish, James Robert, and Allan Taylor: *The Encyclopedia of Ethnic Groups in Hollywood.* New York: Facts On File, 2002.

Smith, Rod. *Jennifer Lopez.* Glenview, Ill.: Pearson, 2000.*

Tracy, Kathleen. *Jennifer Lopez.* Toronto: ECW Press, 2000.

Wheeler, Jill C. *Jennifer Lopez.* Edna, Minn.: Abdo, 2003.*

* Young Adult Book

TELEVISION

Driven (VH1, 2002)

Intimate Portrait (Lifetime, 2002)

J.Lo Revealed (E! Entertainment TV, 2002)

J.Lo Unveiled (E! Entertainment TV, 2002)
PrimeTime with Diane Sawyer (ABC-TV, 2002)

WEBSITES
Absolutely Jennifer Lopez
http://www.absolutely.net/lopez

AllMusic
http://www.allmusic.com

ALMA Awards
http://www.almaawards.com

Diva Jennifer Lopez
http://www.diva-jlo.com

Jennifer Lopez Official Site
http://www.jenniferlopez.com

Sony Music
http://sonymusic.com

INDEX

Page numbers in *italics* indicate illustrations.

ABOUT THE AUTHOR

James Robert Parish, a former entertainment reporter, publicist, and book series editor, is the author of numerous biographies and reference books on the entertainment industry, including: *Katie Couric: TV Newscaster*; *Stan Lee: Comic-Book Writer*; *Twyla Tharp: Choreographer*; *Denzel Washington: Actor*; *Halle Berry: Actor*; *Stephen King: Writer*; *Tom Hanks: Actor*; *Steven Spielberg: Filmmaker*; *Katherine Hepburn: The Untold Story*; *The Hollywood Book of Scandal*; *Whitney Houston*; *The Hollywood Book of Love*; *Hollywood Divas*; *Hollywood Bad Boys*; *The Encyclopedia of Ethnic Groups in Hollywood*; *Jet Li*; *Gus Van Sant*; *The Hollywood Book of Death*; *Whoopi Goldberg*; *Rosie O'Donnell's Story*; *The Unofficial "Murder, She Wrote" Casebook*; *Today's Black Hollywood*; and *Let's Talk! America's Favorite TV Talk Show Hosts*.

Mr. Parish is a frequent on-camera interviewee on cable and network TV for documentaries on the performing arts both in the United States and in the United Kingdom. He resides in Studio City, California. Mr. Parish's Web site is at http://www.jamesrobertparish.com.